Books By Michel Mockers

RENÉ'S WAR
Memoirs of Resistance (1944)

Köchel. 595
A Play in Two Parts

THE BUTTOCKS
of the REPUBLIC
Novel

THE MAGNOLIAS
of the EMPEROR OF CHINA
A history of the process of oil painting

RENE'S WAR

MEMOIRS OF FRENCH RESISTANCE IN WWII

MICHEL MOCKERS

New Dawn Services Inc.
60 East Simpson Avenue
Jackson Wyoming 83001
info@newdawnservices.net

Note From the Publisher

Mr. Mockers has requested that we make an effort to keep the "French-ness" of the story intact. Our attempt to do so has been fraught with difficult choices. Where we felt that the intended meaning might be difficult to understand, we have erred on the side of caution and taken editorial liberties to make his story more accessible. However, where we felt that the storyline was easy to follow, we have left the original telling of the story intact.

Here is an example that may be useful; on page 17 We quote from the text:

"Ah! Pôvre!" Rebuffat said with his strong Provençal accent. "What happens to you?"

In standard American English it would read: Oh, poor boy, what has happened to you?

We hope that you will enjoy Mr. Mockers story and be reminded of the horrible cost of war emotionally, physically, and spiritually.

Michel Mockers' war citation from from The British Government:

Le porteur de la présente est le Sous/Lieutenant Michel
MOCKERS qui a travaillé sous les ordres de notre organisateur
WRESTLER depuis le 1er Mai 1944. Le 6 Juin il organisa lui-
même un maquis qui résistait à une lourde attaque allemande
le 11 Juin. Depuis cette date le Sous/Lieutenant MOCKERS
travaillant toujours sous les ordres de WRESTLER s'occupait
plus particulièrement de toutes les questions financières
concernant tous les maquis compris dans le circuit WRESTLER.

Pendant cette période il fit preuve de grands dons
d'organisation et d'initiative, et son chef en fait des plus
hauts éloges.

Paris. Le 28 Décembre 1944.

Lt.Col.

5

Michel Mockers' war citations from the French Government:

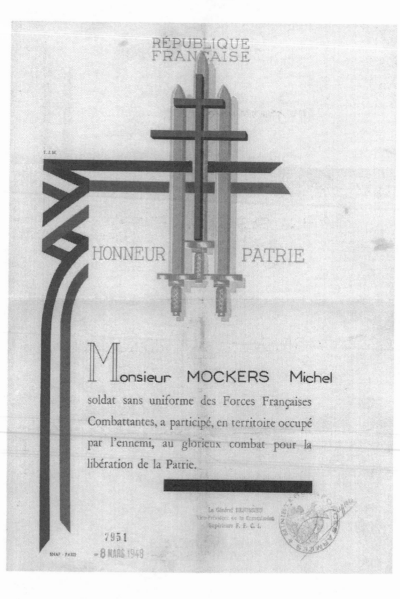

RÉPUBLIQUE FRANÇAISE

Guerre 1939-1945

CITATION

EXTRAIT DE L'ORDRE GENERAL N° 190

Le Colonel ROUSSELIER (RIVIER)
Commandant la 12ème Région Militaire

C I T E

A L'ORDRE DE LA BRIGADE

· ·

M O C K E R S - Lieutenant F.F.I. - Subdivision de Châteauroux -

pour le motif suivant :

" Résistant de la première heure; a travaillé avec la mission an-
" glaise et est devenu intendant des secteurs Nord-Indre. A participé avec cou-
" rage au combat des Souches le 11 juin 1944. A regroupé les maquis dispersés
" et reformé un groupe qu'il a commandé avec ardeur, abnégation et intelligence".

· ·

CES CITATIONS COMPORTENT L'ATTRIBUTION DE LA CROIX DE GUERRE
1939-1945 AVEC ETOILE DE BRONZE .

FAIT A LIMOGES LE 24 MARS 1945

signé: ROUSSELIER

EXTRAIT CERTIFIE CONFORME :

PARIS, le   2 8 MARS 1966
L'Administrateur Civil hors classe BERT
    Chef du Bureau des Décorations,
P.O. Le Commissaire de la Marine CHANALET,

To those who were my companions and especially
those who gave their lives for the freedom of their country.

Introduction

Fifteen thousand Allied airmen whose planes were shot down by the Germans were officially rescued by underground forces in Europe during World War II. If the three Americans that I rescued were still alive, as I am myself in 2008, they would tell you exactly the same story that you will find in some of the following pages.

I invite you to accompany me on my visit to bygone times of World War II, driving with me in my "verboten" car, during the summer of 1944, on roads that crisscrossed our area to see what I saw, and to share with me some intense moments of suspense. I still wonder why, on some occasions, I remained alive to tell you my story, the story of a young man who was labeled "terrorist" by the Germans.

I was not considered to be a freedom fighter but a "terrorist" because I opposed by force what was imposed upon me by force. Of course, "we" were not despicable terrorists killing innocents and blowing up public buildings. We were outlaws living in the woods and attacking all that we could possibly attack, especially German military convoys. We became experienced in appearing, striking, and disappearing. We fought on roads and streets. We blew up all that we could blow up, bridges, railroad tracks, electric railroad lines... If there had been oil pipelines, we would have blown up oil pipelines.

German armies occupied France for four years. For four years, they fought endlessly and uselessly against a growing resistance by "terrorists" who had to be "ground like meat for paté," according to a German leaflet we found on the road. Germans knew every street of every town and village.

The Nazis arrested and tortured individuals, took hostages, tried to locate, and eventually found radios by triangulation, set traps to catch terrorists, and attacked groups of resistance with armed forces. They had all the weapons that armies have, while ours were of the lightest kind. Despite that handicap, the Germans never succeeded in crushing the "resistance." When they arrested or killed one "terrorist," more came in to replace him or her. In my own sector, we were a few people at the beginning, more than two thousand at the end. When people fight for a cause in which they believe, they are ready to give their lives for it, as we were, as I was.

Michel Mockers

Croix de Guerre 1939-1945

RENÉ'S WAR

I was nineteen years old, and my brother Christian was seventeen. The year was 1941. Christian and I had left Paris and crossed the "line of demarcation" separating occupied France from "free" France. The line was strictly controlled by the Germans, but we had forded the river serving as the "line" in that part of France south of Paris. We had spent our last two summer vacations before the war there, and knew the area well enough to keep clear of German checkpoints. Far away from the line of demarcation, we were in Provence where German soldiers were not swarming around. To be exact, we were at "La Sainte Beaume" in the heights above the town of Aubagne.

The site is grandiose. A narrow and elongated plateau is dominated by a seven-mile-long mass of rock that ends up abruptly in a one-thousand-foot cliff above the buildings of a large hostelry for pilgrims visiting the place where Mary Magdalena is supposed to have ended her life in a grotto located inside the cliff. At the foot of the cliff, stretches an indigenous forest of green trees contrasting with the typically Provençal dry aspect of the rest of the plateau. Before reaching the hostelry, a few houses complete the landscape.

The hostelry was directed by one of our uncles, Uncle Peter, a Dominican and brother of my mother. The bedrooms were far from luxurious, but the beds were comfortable. The food was simple and hardly enough in quantity and proteins. A little more would have been OK, but there was no little more. The main items on the menu were potatoes vaguely browned in only God knew what type of oil, and pancakes of chickpea flour lacking butter, heavy cream, or even milk. The hostelry owned a large flock of sheep and, once in a while, one was chosen to become the lamb sacrificed for the survival of the residents. Christian and I were giving a hand here and there, helping to kill the sheep or run the generator that provided the buildings with light, but doing really nothing, and with nothing intelligent to do in front of us.

From La Sainte Beaume, there was no possibility to attend any school or college. To repel my doomsday feeling, I drew daily and strengthened in my mind my decision to be an artist, but it seemed to me that it would be absolutely impossible under German occupation. They had defeated us so fast that they seemed invincible and installed in France forever.

We were not for long in the "free France." The Germans invaded it in November. One of their main intentions was to capture the French navy anchored or at dock in the military harbor at Toulon. They did not capture the fleet since it had been scuttled by its sailors, and the Germans were again everywhere.

Day after day, my brother and I discussed the situation until, three months later, sitting together outside on a big round stone in a warm early morning sun, we made the decision to leave La Sainte Beaume and fight the Germans. How to fight the Germans was another problem. We also agreed that we would not stay together to avoid putting two eggs in the same basket. We did not want to follow the same path, go through the same ordeals, and eventually meet the same death. Consequently, one of us would try to join the French free forces in North Africa. The other would stay in France and fight by whatever means he would find.

Both of us having sternly declared that we had no preference, we decided to let fate choose for us. Christian took a coin out of his pocket. Face, outside; tail, inside. Up and down went the coin. Christian was to leave France, and I was to stay inside. Two or three days later, Uncle Peter and I told Christian goodbye when he stepped onto the bus leaving La Sainte Beaume for Aubagne. From Aubagne, he would have to find transportation to the Spanish border, Spain being the only way out of France, to reach North Africa. It was the last glance that we had of each other, and I must confess that I was close to crying when the bus disappeared at the first turn in the road.

So, I was left by my brother at La Sainte Beaume. There I was unable to make a fast decision on what to do next. Leaving La Sainte Beaume was heart breaking for me. I loved the blue sky of Provence and the smell of the plateau. I had seen under my window that opened three feet above the ground something that I had never seen before, never saw after, and certainly will never see again. I counted them. There were sixteen rabbits gathered together. The Provençal type is small, as Provence is a country where rich grass is scarce. Those have the smell of thyme and lavender. Seated in the moonlight, they formed a perfect circle. They remained in that position for about five minutes, and left. I waited for hours during the following nights to see if the rabbits would come back, but they never did. When I told my story to other people, they cried humbug.

More credible was my pal the little donkey. Each day he carried a packsaddle containing some food and mail to a hermit who was living next to the grotto. That donkey was the cutest donkey, the most patient, and with the smartest donkey's brain under his long ears, but he was also the most stubborn when he refused to do something. He was waiting for the word "go" to leave the hostelry for the grotto, all by himself. I accompanied the donkey once in a while for the pleasure of walking through the forest. I have not mentioned, yet, that this forest is the most extraordinary forest in the world because of the diversity of its trees that remain green on a plateau scorched by the sun. Snakes are abundant in Provence, but from man's memory, none has ever been seen in the forest. It is said that their absence is a gift from Mary-Magdalena who banned them from nesting under the trees.

Those sentimental pretexts, made of small nothings like love for a donkey or the freshness of a forest, represented only an illusory life buoy. They were desperate attempts by a lost soul contemplating the disaster engulfing his life at making believe that they were valid reasons to stay there instead of facing reality beyond the plateau. La Sainte Beaume resembled the last cigarette of a man going to be executed, a last glimpse at a disappearing world of peace before plunging into the intellectual, material, and physical horror of war. I could not stand the idea of war, but I also knew perfectly well that we had to fight if we wanted our freedom back. I had to expel from my mind every reason that would diminish my determination.

Of course, I could have remained there as long as I wanted, exchanging some work for bread and bed but, after having definitively made up my mind on the necessity of war, La Sainte Beaume started resembling, in my mind a place on another planet populated by rabbits, donkeys, and nice people acting as if there was no war. It was, in any case, far from any possible action, and Uncle Peter agreed with me on that. He was the exception from the general disinterested attitude of the place. He was discreetly conducting his personal war, but I had no role within it.

My Dominican uncle had created a school of hotel management for women in the second building of the hostelry. The school was officially sponsored by the local government, and the teaching was very serious. The teachers were all women and so were the forty students, aged fifteen to twenty. Falsifying books, records, and identifications, teachers and students resided in the school all year long. They were Jewish girls and women whose parents were in hiding or had been deported. I learned afterward that the Gestapo had finally figured out what was going on in the "school," and had made a date to wipe it out.

It happened that their date for the operation coincided with the day when the Allied forces landed in Provence. That day, the Germans had more to do elsewhere than take care of a few Jewish girls. The operation never took place, and Uncle Peter saw the hand of God in that occurrence.

Thus, it was no longer my plan to live forever at La Sainte Beaume. The forest and the rocks offered a sure retreat if the Germans showed their noses on that route going nowhere but, precisely for that reason, they were not going to show their noses at La Sainte Beaume, a piece of France that was of absolutely no interest to them. Except for the girls in my uncle's school, there was nobody of my age around. The girls were untouchable, and would be of no help.

One channel was open to me that was, so far, out of the reach of Germans, and gathered only boys my age, the "Chantiers de Jeunesse." Perhaps I would find there a nucleus of guys sharing my desire to do something? I would need no money, as I would be paid, a few pennies a month, but paid and fed. The "Chantiers" wanted to be some kind of army without guns substituting for the real army. The discipline tried to look like military discipline. The uniform was green, and because of the temperature in the South of France, shorts replaced pants. My shoes had certainly been resoled ten times. Above those shoes, a pair of absolutely ridiculous leather leggings squeezed my legs. Wearing them,

I looked like a gladiator who had missed his century. The food was meager but, at least, there was some food.

We were lodged in a big hotel at Hyères, one of those hotels built at the end of the nineteenth century to welcome the British tourists who were spending the winter months on the French Mediterranean coast. I had been there seven months, singing every morning the exalted verses of the hymn to the Marshal Pétain,

Marshal, here we are
In front of you,
The Savior of France....

when, one evening, the Germans let us know that, within one week, all those who could not prove that they were agricultural workers, would volunteer to go to work in German factories to help at the final victory. One minute after the opening the next morning, it was impossible to enter into the post office. Everyone in our Hotel-Chantier de Jeunesse wanted to become a certified country worker, including me who counted on an affidavit signed by the sheep that I had not slaughtered to be considered as a farming specialist. It was basically the meaning of the telegram that I sent to Uncle Peter after queuing for at least two hours.

The telegram was of no use. The next evening, we learned that, agricultural specialists or not, we were all volunteering to go to Germany. With no exception, however, the Germans did not move fast enough, at least in our area. In less than twenty-four hours, all the birds flew away.

Early in the morning, a small train joined Hyères to Toulon with no I.D. control. That morning, half the Chantier de Jeunesse stormed the train. The other half was already lost in the landscape. From Toulon to Aubagne, movement was easy and without I.D. control. The Germans could not be everywhere. After Toulon, I found myself alone. The others had evaporated. I knew that I was going to be considered a deserter by the Vichy authorities and a warrant would be issued for my arrest. I needed to change my name and age as soon as possible. The only person able to provide me with a new card of identification and something to eat in the immediacy was again Uncle Peter. I pondered walking from Aubagne to La Sainte Beaume.

Without utilizing the road that was potentially dangerous, I had a tough and long journey in front of me, going up and up the stones of steep slopes to reach la Sainte Beaume. I would not arrive before the middle of the night.

Emboldened by the previous lack of controls in local public transportation, I chose to take the risk of using the daily bus from Aubagne to La Sainte Beaume, supposing that it was not controlled. Rebuffat, the driver, was an old friend devoted to my uncle who fed him at lunchtime before he took a nap on the back seat of his bus parked in the shadow of the only big tree in front of the hostelry. The bus was leaving Aubagne in the morning to go up the "mountain," and leaving La Sainte Beaume in the afternoon to go back to Aubagne at sea level.

"Ah! Pôvre!" Rebuffat said with his strong Provençal accent. "What happens to you?"

I explained my situation and why I had to go and see my uncle. Rebuffat's comment was that there was no problem. He would be happy to help me. I had arrived just on time to take the bus. "Take the bus" was a way of speaking. "There is a post of control," Rebuffat declared. He certainly saw an alteration in the color of my face. "Don't worry," he said immediately. "I always carry a lot of things on the roof of the bus, especially for your uncle. There is a

17

tarpaulin on top. You disappear under it and we pass the German control." I supposed that he knew what he was saying about the German control.

The thirty-passenger bus was not a prehistoric machine, but it ran on the gas produced by a big wood burning apparatus, a "gasogene" hanging on its back. I climbed the back ladder to reach the top and discovered that I was not alone. Another guy was already there. Much older than me, long legs in some kind of a blue jeans, very thin but with a joyous grin, and harboring overgrown gray hair, he looked like a happy hippie. We did not talk but disappeared under the tarpaulin, strategically surrounded by baskets and suitcases. We were certainly invisible from the ground.

At the exit from Aubagne, the bus stopped for the German control. When we left after the check, I managed to have a look between two baskets at the road behind us. The German soldier was an old man with a nice potbelly, certainly very glad to be stationed in the south of France, but not inclined to climb up the ladder to check the roof. He let the bus pass without verifying the papers of the passengers who filled only half of it.

As soon as the road started to go up and the bus to slow down, because the gas produced by the wood was not very powerful, we came out from under the tarpaulin. The bus' speed was not much faster on the winding road than the pace of a walking man. We systematically inspected the baskets. We found a basket of tomatoes addressed to the hostelry. A few of them constituted the breakfast of two starving men. We rearranged the basket in such a way that our larceny was not too visible.

I remained at La Sainte Beaume for the time necessary for my uncle to provide me with a fake identity card. I was no longer myself. From now on, I had to live under the skin of someone named René Belleau, born in a town where I had never put my feet, and three years younger than I was. I now belonged to a parallel society where false was becoming true and true was becoming false. A few days later, René Belleau took the bus to Aubagne, but this time as a passenger confident in his new identity, and with a small provision of money put in his pocket by his uncle.

Aubagne to Marseilles was a smooth bus ride, surprisingly with no control. I had to take a train at Marseilles to go north. That was the main line from Marseilles to Paris. With no specific goal in mind, I had decided to go and see if there would be more opportunities in the area where my grandmother was living. That was precisely where Christian and I had forded the "line," countryside of fields and small woods or forests, farms, and villages, and not too far away from several important towns.

Taking a train was easier said than done. The station's platform, with no train in sight, was overcrowded. I thought that many of those people would never be able to board the train. More than two hours later, the train backed slowly to stop in front of us. Marseilles being a terminal, the train could go no farther than the end of the platform. A human tidal wave assaulted the cars. Pieces of luggage were thrown through the windows to people already inside. The next problem of their owners was to manage to rejoin their luggage. Some people certainly saw their luggage leaving without them.

I was lucky. When the train stopped backing, the open door of a car stood in front of me. The best I could do, nonetheless, when I finally succeeded at putting my feet inside the car, was to stand at the open door. There was no way to go farther inside. As traveling without any luggage would have eventually looked suspicious, I carried a small suitcase that I kept between my feet. The door could not be closed before we left the station, and I traveled for at least one hour in the wind created by the speed of the train. I started to get cold. Moving inch by inch, we finally closed the door, but standing up remained the only possible position. There were three people squeezed in the toilet and half a dozen squeezed in the flexible connection between our car and the next. People were patient and trying to help one another. After a long while, perhaps with no other reason than refusing to drown hopelessly in a sea of absurdity, I impulsively did something that I would have never ventured to do before. I put my left arm around the shoulders of a woman standing on my left. I saw on her profile that she smiled before leaning against me.

The train stopped four times. Fewer people came on board than left, which gave us enough room to evacuate the toilet, allowing its use. If it created a permanent movement of passengers in great need, it did not give anybody else any more room to move, including the young woman at my side and myself. It was impossible to sit on the floor or on a suitcase, and everybody remained standing all night.

It was daylight when the train reached my destination. I managed to face her. She looked tired, but she had beautiful and wide dark eyes, very dark hair, almost black, and a nice face with appealing lips. We had not exchanged one word during the whole night, but I had been troubled for hours by feeling her body pressed against mine. "Are you sure that you want to go to Paris?" I asked with no logical reason, just before the train stopped, in a sudden impulse that overcame my natural timidity. I hoped without hope that she would say no. I would take her by the hand and we would live together a warlike romantic adventure, my first romantic adventure. I was daydreaming. "I have to," she answered, breaking my dream. She smiled. I thought we were both pathetic. "In other circumstances," she said. She put her lips on mine. "Goodbye," she said very gently, "and take good care of yourself."

I had not even asked her for her name. Stepping down from the car, my sentimental instincts were all of a sudden cooled down when I saw the soldiers on the platform. My heart froze when I also saw two plainclothes Gestapo agents checking the papers of every passenger at the exit. I had no alternative. As cool as I could be, but my heart bouncing under my shirt, I presented my open card to one of them. The man looked at it and then at me for seconds that seemed an eternity. He folded my identification card and gave it back to me without a word.

They called it a village, but it was not really a village, rather a hamlet with a church, a school, and no store, a point on a small road. But let's call it "village." The village was standing on top of a lazy hill. When coming into it from the west, the road faced three attached houses and forked in front of them to form a small triangular plaza. On the left side of the triangle was a small house where I now lived with my grandmother. The house was surrounded by a garden. Next to the garden was a small church with a pointed belfry, where a single bell announced mass, baptisms, weddings, and funerals. The church windows were not made of stained glass but held patterns of small lozenges of white glass. After passing the church, the road sloped down to reach the river bridge, a few kilometers farther. There stood, across the bridge, a real village with several stores.

On the right side of the fork was a farmhouse. After the farmhouse, on the left side of that road was the schoolhouse. After the schoolhouse, the road wandered into the landscape. The school had one classroom that occupied half of the one-story building. All the houses in the village were of one-story. Since the beginning of the war, there had been no students and no teacher. The school was closed. Father Durand occupied the other half of the building, two rooms and a kitchen. It had become the church's rectory.

A graduate from Salzburg University, Father Durand had wanted to be a missionary in Africa, but responsible for his mother's care at that time, he had not been allowed to realize his wish. He found himself trapped in that rectory at the beginning of the war, certainly very far from the excitement of a university or adventures on African savannas.

A country boy, he knew all the farmers around and was at ease with them, but one could see on his face, and perceive in his eyes, his longing for an unachieved dream. Put in simple terms, one could figure out that he was not completely happy.

He was the reason my grandmother was living there. He was an old friend of my family, through vacations many years ago, and had remained in contact, and when my parents thought that it would be better for my grandmother to live outside Paris, they called on him. He found the little house for her. My parents had an apartment in Paris but they did not reside permanently in Paris. Queuing for hours to obtain a small piece of bread would be impossible for my grandmother without help. Being there, Father Durand could watch over her. She would always have enough to eat. Unlike Paris and the big cities, food was not a problem in places like the village.

The house was a small stone house with a low attic. Inside were one large room and two bedrooms. It was the summer residence of "Parisians" who had asked Father Durand to rent it if he could, and to keep the rent money for when they would come back from overseas after the war. The house was furnished. My grandmother, who was my maternal grandmother, had only brought a few personal items and books. She was saying that, getting old, she was abandoning serious reading and she had a collection of Simenon's detective stories at the head of her bed.

Issued from one of the oldest French families with two faraway-in-the-past ancestors buried somewhere around Jerusalem during the First Crusade, my grandmother had kept noble manners. She could not eat a peach without a fork and a knife. My mother also told me that, when she was young, my grandmother was a very attractive socialite with a permanent crowd of would-be-suitors. She was always dressed in the latest "avant-garde" fashion to the dismay, sometimes the horror, of local bigots. She had finally married an industrialist who died relatively young from the lung cancer of a heavy smoker. He left her two small factories that she sold afterward.

My grandmother had a horrible tragedy in her life when, after renting a second floor, large and comfortable apartment at Auteuil, she opened the double door of a balcony. Robert was four years old and Gerard two. The boys started playing, jumping the one step from the balcony into the room. Neighbors said that they would never forget the scream of his mother, my grandmother, when she saw her little Robert, who had disappeared after a second of inattention, lying on the sidewalk.

An ambulance took him and his mother to the Hôpital de la Pitié. The little boy died nine days later. The hospital's doctor, who received him, accused his mother of being an irresponsible mother, and the chief of police accused her of having voluntarily murdered her child.

Those were not the thoughts that went through my head when I reached the door of her house. My grandmother was now seventy-two years old. Contrary to her usual appearance of dignity, she went absolutely wild when she recognized me knocking at the open door. "Is that really you?" Joy left her almost speechless, her elaborate chignon got loose, her white hair flowing on her shoulders, and it seemed to me that the light-blue color of her eyes turned into a deep-sea blue. She opened her arms. "Come upon my heart," she said. "Thank God, you are here! I am not going to be alone anymore."

Father Durand's reception was also more than warm hearted. He was in his forties, dressed in a black cassock, a friendly face with dark hair and blue eyes. I was very happy to see him again. Between my grandmother and him, I was not completely lost in unknown territory. I could count on both of them, and I felt better. I told both of them that, René Belleau being my name on my identity card, they should call me René in front of anyone else. Just in case…. You never can tell!

On the recommendation of Father Durand, I was immediately hired by a farmer that everybody called "P'tit Louis," Lil' Louis. Nobody knew why he was nicknamed P'tit Louis. He was a big man, always joyous and happy. He owned a small farm inherited from an uncle, and the farm was enough for him and his wife, Annette. Annette was an attractive little brunette as quick as the silver "goujons" that we were fishing for in the river while on vacation.

Annette was my age, P'tit Louis a little older. They had a baby girl to whom I was singing "Le Petit Prince" to put her asleep. One of P'tit Louis' best qualities was that he was not a workaholic. Annette was often obliged to give him a push. On those occasions, she would lose her smile and scream after him that he was a lousy guy, lazy bum, and that she did not know why she had married him. In such circumstance, P'tit Louis would leave in a hurry, going straight to the stables to clean them or disappearing with a tool on his shoulders in the direction of the field of potatoes. Her anger would fade immediately, as if by enchantment, and a smile would be back on her face.

Nothing altered P'tit Louis' joyous natural disposition and his favorite moment of the day remained imperturbably dinnertime. I definitely shared his preference. Many town people would have considered our meals as extreme luxuries: soup with or without meat, boiled potatoes with raw onions, goat cheese, and wine.

If I give all those details, it is because I was going to work at P'tit Louis' farm for a long period of time.

When reaching the farm, the farmhouse was on the left, a low house with an attic accessible by an outside ladder. Entering the house, there was a large room both kitchen and dining room. A large stove, whose smoke pipe disappeared in the chimney's conduit, obstructed the chimney. A long table with six wooden chairs occupied a whole side of the room that opened on two bedrooms. It was as if all the houses around were one large room and two bedrooms. A dairy room where Annette prepared her cheeses completed the house on the right. It was accessible only from outside. On the left side of the house was a vegetable garden protected from the goats by a high latticework fence.

Separated from the farmhouse, at a right angle, a large building sheltered two horse stalls, a stable for six cows, and a space for the goats. P'tit Louis had two horses. He permanently complained that they represented too many mouths to feed, but he had to keep them both, one for work reasons, "Fierce," and the other, "Coquette," for sentimental reasons.

When I met her, "Coquette" was twenty-seven years old, a very advanced age for a horse. Her longevity resided, with no doubt, in the fact that she had never worked during her whole life. On Sunday morning, P'tit Louis' uncle and his wife rode to the small church. Late in the afternoon, his uncle rode to the "village at the bridge" to play a few card games with his friends, and get drunk. Late at night, with a slap on her buttock by the uncle's friends, she knew exactly what her duty was. She crossed the bridge, turning right at the end of it, going up the hill at a nice canter, turning left in front of the church to take the road on the left, passing the schoolhouse, and turning left again to take the path to the farm. There, she stopped in front of the door and waited usually until morning, when her master was sober enough to unharness her.

Next to the stables was an open space with heavy timber supporting a second floor, barn like, which ran the length of the building, and where hay and bags of grain for the animals were stored. Part of it was reserved for the bags of wheat for sale after the harvest, the bags for the next sowings, and the bags for the annual German requisition. The Germans never came to pick up their share of the bounty, of course, but the French authorities did. Cheating was admitted to a certain extent, but reprisals were always hanging over everybody's head.

The day after my arrival, I made the first friend of my age, Marc, the grandson of the farmers who owned the farm at the entrance to the village. Father Durand had taken me to meet Marc's family. In the evening, Marc and I were waiting at the "rectory" with Father Durand for another boy to show up. A bottle of white wine was on the table with four glasses and a deck of cards. When Eugene knocked at the door, Father Durand exhibited a broad smile. "Now," he said, "We are enough players for a real bridge game." Addressing me, he added, "I taught bridge to those two. I hope you play, because with only three-players, bridge is no fun."

It has to be noted that entertainment was scarce. Most people had a radio that they were usually hiding after listening to the Beethoven "Boum, Boum, Boum, Boum," followed by "Ici Radio Londres. The French talk to the French." The talk was preceded by a series of "personal messages." They were encrypted messages. "The carrots are cooked" had no meaning for those who were not involved in the cooking of those carrots. Radio owners were paranoid, always afraid that someone would hear them listening to London and denounce them. Out of pure patriotism, nobody listened to the German radio, except, perhaps, those who were deliberately pro-German. Once in a while, London denounced by name active "collaborators" in towns, sometimes in mere villages.

Beside those few minutes of radio aimed at lifting the morale of occupied France, entertainment in the village consisted of two card games: bridge at the rectory with Father Durand and the initiated, and "belote," a much simpler game that necessitated the ritual invasion with no previous notice of one farm in the vicinity. Father Durand usually joined the invading party. The farmers were never reluctant to open their doors and put wine and cards on the table. Their evenings lacked entertainment and they were happy when something unexpected broke the monotony. Good manners directed those evenings, and nobody, absolutely nobody, ever got drunk. Getting drunk was a different type of enterprise that did not happen very often, and, when it did, it was in no way prejudicial to anyone.

Only once was I, in the company of Marc, Eugene, and a fourth young man named Pierre, officially drunk – but with attenuating circumstances. During the winter of 1943, a snowstorm left three feet of snow behind. Three feet of snow was absolutely abnormal in our area. It was also the day when help was asked to carry out the funeral of a ten-year-old boy. The problem was that, with the snow, no horse could pull a carriage up to the top of the hill, six kilometers away, where the church and cemetery stood. The solution was to use a light four-wheeled carriage that could be pulled and pushed by several men. Father Durand, who was also the pastor of that small parish, volunteered our help without asking us. At seven in the morning, we were on the road that led in an almost straight line to a church visible far away in the morning sun. Nature was silent under the snow that sparkled around us in millions of glittering dots under the sunrays. The chariot was light, as was the coffin, rather the box, of a ten-year-old boy, but we had not pulled and pushed the cart more than ten minutes when we were hailed by the people of the first farm along the way. "Eh, guys!" they shouted from the farmhouse, "You cannot go on like that. Come and have something hot. You need it." We doubted that we needed it, but it would have been very impolite to refuse the invitation. We did not stay more than ten minutes and went back to the road, comforted by a beverage that was as black as coffee but was not coffee, and cut, as they say over there, with almost the same amount of alcohol. I suppose that we lost completely track of time and events after the sixth farm. We nevertheless succeeded at reaching the church where the parents, a few other people, and Father Durand waited desperately for us. It was said, afterward, that we had formed a quartet to sing the "Dies Irae" (Day of Wrath) and a few responses. I never remembered singing the "Dies Irae." I only hoped that we had not made too joyous its habitual mourning and angry tone.

I was uncomfortable when I thought that I had not come there to play bridge or learn how to fill up a tumbrel of manure, harness "Fierce" to it, and spread the manure on a field. I never understood why that horse was named

"Fierce." It was as sweet as a lamb and as lazy as an adder, adders having the reputation of being very lazy, especially when resting in the sun.

I knew that the apparent calm would not last forever, and I waited for something to happen. It did by surprise one Sunday afternoon of late March. Marc, who had many connections in the area, because he had been born a few kilometers away, had succeeded in inviting two girls from the "village at the bridge" to spend the afternoon with us. It was a sunny but fresh day. The four of us took the path down to the river but we stopped midway. A nice patch of grass, protected by young trees from inquiring eyes traveling on the road, was the ideal spot for laying out the blanket we carried. The freshness of March's grass made the blanket a necessity. Marc's grandmother had baked a pie and we had taken two bottles of wine with us.

We were having a good time. We were flirting decently with the girls who expected no less from us. My elected companion was the daughter of a bricklayer. She was nice looking, according to my appreciation of the moment, and she had certainly put on her best skirt, blouse, and jacket. I was engaged in a double-meaning conversation with her to find out if I could meet her again in the near future when we heard a voice, the voice of a kid, calling, "Marc! Marc!"

Marc answered. A young boy, maybe twelve years old, rushed to us. "Your grand-mother told me that you were gone in the direction of the river." He had run all the way. "Calm down," Marc said. "What's up?"

"Daniel has been arrested by a German patrol. They took him away."

I had never met Daniel, but Marc knew him. It was a stroke of thunder in our serene sky. The girls were already on their feet. Marc told them to go back home. We would call for them another time. According to the boy, the arrest had happened only a few kilometers away while Daniel was bicycling on a road that we considered almost as our personal property. It was too late to react and, beside, to do what? We were in no condition to react but, so far, the Germans had never patrolled our small roads and made any arrest. We went back in a hurry to Marc's farm. Daniel's arrest was full of significance and consequences. That evening, Marc and I declared our personal war on Germany.

Our first act of war consisted of going to church the next Sunday. There were usually several boys, more or less our age, attending church on Sunday morning. Marc and I always attended, considering that it was the least we could do for Father Durand. Coming regularly to mass on Sunday were several farmer couples, husbands and wives, two or three very young girls who disappeared as soon as they were out of church, and also a young girl, who was always leaning her bicycle against the right side wall of the church, leaving almost as fast as the two or three other very young girls after the mass. She was a nice-looking girl with blond hair and surprisingly green eyes. I thought that she had beautiful eyes but, so far, our conversation had been limited to "Hello!" She was definitely not the talking type. My grandmother also attended, wearing a beautiful "Italian straw hat" that two indefinite artificial flowers ornamented. After mass, she was always hurrying home to prepare a Sunday lunch.

Marc and I decided to go to mass on that Sunday despite the menace of patrolling Germans. We wanted to see if some of the boys that we had already met on previous Sundays would be there. We supposed that they would because everybody knew about Daniel, and the boys would come to talk about his arrest. If that proved to be true, we could test them to find out if they would participate in our local war against Germany to avenge Daniel.

After mass, and the departure of the farmers, of the two or three very young girls who always disappeared as soon as they were out of church, and of my grandmother, two boys remained, beside Marc, Eugene, myself, and the blond girl. Father Durand introduced her as "Michelle." He told me later that she was twenty years old. They talked about nothing else but Daniel's arrest. The conversation going nowhere, I got impatient and, all of a sudden, I spoke. Using direct words, I announced our project of creating a Resistance group. It was now public knowledge that the Germans were chasing all the young men to send them to Germany under the title of Service du Travail Obligatoire (mandatory work service) (STO). In any case, every young man was now living under the threat of being arrested, eventually on the suspicion of being a member of the underground. The only solution was to vanish and to wage war against the Germans. Practicalities would have to be discussed. For now, everyone would stay home and avoid wandering on the roads. Everyone had nevertheless to be ready for any eventuality. They should discuss the matter with their parents if they were living with them.

It naturally came to my mind to add, "And we should not be standing like this, in the middle of the road, perfect prey for the Germans. Pick a name that will be yours from now on. No real name, no identification. And, sorry to say, Father, we will not come to your Sunday mass anymore."

"War is war, and you are right," Father Durand acquiesced. "From now on, mass would be too dangerous for you." But he added with a smile, "And so would bridge."

After our common declaration of war on Germany, things went faster than I could have hoped. We did some recruiting. I had now twelve men including my friend Marc. I loved Marc who was a cool guy, always with a joke or a saying, adaptable to any situation. The twelve were still living at home but ready to leave. Michelle often passed by the rectory to learn if she had to contact "the boys." I had met her there only once or twice because she came when I was still working at P'tit Louis'. On those occasions, my conversations with her had been of the least size, as, "The meeting is on for Friday as usual."

"Goodbye, then," she would say. "I'll take care of it.. as usual."

In one hour, pedaling fast, she could contact all of us. We held our weekly meeting at the rectory. We were talking about our desire to do something, but what? We still had neither weapons, nor the slightest idea of what action we could take. In accord with Father Durand, I imposed those meetings to keep our group intact. Michelle seemed happy to be with us but she was definitely not of the talking type.

I was desperately trying to establish contact with other groups – if they existed. Until now, I had been unsuccessful. Once in a while, in the quietness of my grandmother's house, I wondered if I was living in a real world, or floating into some kind of dream. Even the presence of my grandmother in that small house in that hamlet seemed unreal. I always came directly from the farm to her house after my dinner with Annette and P'tit Louis, often bringing her some vegetables or eggs, sometimes a chicken. Annette was not stingy. Then, I would often leave my grandmother to go and play bridge at the rectory. In the morning, as early as I might get up, she would already be preparing my breakfast.

One evening, Father Durand waited for me on my way back from the farm. "Come in," he said. "I have some very important information for you. Being a priest, I can only see the hand of Providence in what I am going to tell you...if it is true." We went inside. Father Durand told me that, according to a personal source, a small group of three or four people had started to use the guardhouse of the "castle" as headquarters.

"Headquarters of what?" he added, "I don't know. I understood that they are not French but British. Where are they coming from? What do they want to do? Nobody knows. You have to contact them. But we must be very prudent. Let me be sure that my information is correct and that we are not dealing with disguised Germans. Everything is possible. You are the only one to whom I report this news."

I went back home very excited but determined to keep silent as long as I did not have more information from Father Durand. Two days later, the priest waited for me again on my way back from the farm.

"The information seems to be correct," he said. "You should go and make contact."

"At this point," I answered, "I am ready to take risks. We cannot go on like this, playing tin soldiers. I am fed up. Where are they?"

Father Durand told me. "I know where it is," I said. "It is not far at all. If what you say is true, it is the contact that we needed from the beginning. If they were British, they certainly play bridge, but I don't believe they came here to play bridge. I'll go first thing tomorrow, and will let you know immediately."

I never asked Father Durand who his contacts were. The following day, he let me know that I was expected at the guardhouse of the "castle." On the north part of the vast forest that we called "the woods" and close to the north-south road that crossed the river at the "bridge of the village," stood an iron gate and a guardhouse. The gate opened onto an alley leading to the "castle," and farther on, to the "dependencies."

I passed by "my" farm to tell P'tit Louis that I had an important meeting and would be late for work. Then I hurried toward the guardhouse. When I arrived, the guard, who shook hands with me, showed me an exterior staircase and an open door on a second floor. The guard introduced himself as Armand. Leather boots and jacket, cap on his head, only his double-barreled gun was missing from his shoulder for his role as "garde-chasse" in Renoir's *The Rules of the Game (La Règle du Jeu)*.

I climbed the stairs to face a man in his thirties, tall, chestnut haired with brown eyes, a face that could fit a university professor or a liberal profession.

"Come in!" he said. "We were expecting you."
Inside were two other people, a woman and a man. The woman was tall, with a thin but firm face, also in her early thirties, blond with light blue eyes, and something that I could not define at first sight. The other man was a dark haired, sturdy man who bore a vague resemblance to Popeye the Sailor Man, without the pipe.

"You don't know who we are," the woman said. She had a slight British accent. The indefinable something was that she represented the image – maybe the cliché – of the typical good looking British woman, and I liked her accent. It proved, at least, that the information about the origin of the group was correct. "My name is Mary," she said. "This is Peter, my adjutant, and Thomas, my radio operator. We are the members of a British mission in charge of this area. We are here, among other things, to help the resistance, if there is one. We know that you already have a small group of men, and a woman, Michelle. We have to start somewhere, from scratch if necessary, but with you and your group, we don't start completely from scratch. Let's see what we can do together."

She was speaking a perfect French with her slight British accent. It was more than evident that I was dealing with the right people. Mary knew what she was talking about. She promised to provide me in the future with all that was necessary to operate against the Germans. When everything was organized, and when the time came, we would act. For the present, things would remain as they were. I should keep in contact with her and give her all the information I could gather. In order to simplify our relationship, we would only talk about "the mission" when talking about the "British" mission.

"Come back to see me in one week," Mary told me before I left.

I felt good. It was finally happening. I went directly to the rectory to give Father Durand a complete report on my meeting with the mission. "We are in business," Father Durand said after I finished talking. "It may be a while before something really happens, but we are in business! We have to contact our people to give them the good news. Let's have a meeting here tomorrow night. I will ask Michelle to ask everyone to come without telling them why. We will have to ask them for absolute secrecy before we can tell them what the meeting is about."

"OK!" I said. "In the meantime, I go back to work at P'tit Louis'."

That night, I told most of the story to my grandmother. Most, that is forgetting details that, in fact, she had no need to know. She had her usual reaction of full support by quoting again the so-said motto of the family, "Let's go on, anyway!"

We held our meeting at the rectory. All together, counting Father Durand, Michelle, and me, we were fifteen people in front of fifteen glasses of wine. I had brought one bottle, Marc one, and Father Durand always had in reserve several bottles of mass wine that could be used in case of unrelated emergencies.

After unanimous "Cheers," I asked everyone to swear that no word of our work would come out of this room. And Father Durand added, a little too dramatically, which happened to him once in a while, "You swear to God, and who does not keep his word will go to hell!" Apparently, he did not include Michelle, forgetting to use the pronoun "her."

I explained that we had been in touch with a British mission, without telling where and how. All they needed to know, for the moment, was that we would be provided in the future with weapons and jobs. "In the meantime, everyone stays home, ready to go any time for anything."

The news electrified the atmosphere. In immediate absence of enemies to kill, we killed a few more bottles of wine before ending the meeting and dispersing into the night.

Passing the door of the rectory, I put my hand on Michelle's arm to stop her. "Can you give me one second?" I asked her. "Michelle," I went on, "you are the one who knows where everyone lives. Would you accept being our permanent liaison officer, if I can call you so?"

"Haven't I been doing it, so far?" There was a surprising hint of brusqueness in her voice. She was to be handled with caution, I thought. But she added, almost mockingly, "Yes, boss!"

"I am no boss!"

"Oh, yes, you are!" She was now very serious. "They are already obeying you because you are the most educated and the smartest of them all. You had better be prepared for the future, whatever it will be."

If she thought that I was smart, as she had said, she was smarter than I was. Until that minute, I had let things go by themselves without philosophizing much about them, but she was opening an abyss under my feet.

"Thank you!" I said.

"You're welcome!"

"That's not what I mean!" I said.

"I know, but you cannot help it!"

She smiled and disappeared in the night. We had never talked so much.

One week later, I was back at the "mission." Mary had navigated along the border of the woods with the help of the guard in search of a field that could be used for parachuting supplies. An auxiliary problem was the storage of the supplies and the concealing of the containers.

There was a vast pond that we all knew, not far away, which could absorb lots of containers. The pond was deep enough, the water dark and dirty enough, and enough trees leaned over it to absorb the containers without surviving traces, even to the eyes of the small German spy plane that flew over the area almost every morning. Caches would be found to store arms and ammunition.

Mary had in mind a field that seemed appropriate and was relatively protected against searching eyes by its surroundings. She told me that she had transmitted its coordinates to London. She had to wait for a reconnaissance plane to take pictures of it and for London's approval. If approved, we would be able to receive a basic load of weapons, ammunition, and a few other items that she expected, such as a portable power generator for the radio. She would need the help of my whole group for the operation.

That day came. My men had to be ready for the following night. The meeting point was an enormous oak standing alone in the middle of a meadow bordering the road at the end of the woods. The meeting was not under the tree, but straight ahead on the other side of the meadow, behind bushes.

I picked up Marc after leaving my grandmother's. We passed the farm and the schoolhouse. Midnight was too late to catch sight of lights from the few farms scattered around. They were small farms with fields or meadows bordered by hedgerows and trees. The cows were in their stables and the farmers in their beds. Reduced to the dimension of the hamlet, the earth seemed immobilized in a no-time zone. The night, a clear and peaceful night in May, was one of those nights without moonlight but with all the stars shining in the sky.

We had a limited view of the road. We were walking fast, making as little noise as possible, and listening intensely to catch any noise other than our own. After a while, we knew that someone was walking in front of us. We also knew that it was one of us. Only one of my men could walk on that dirt road, at that time of the night, and it was not the sound of German boots. Besides, German soldiers never went solo. They were always a minimum of two, and certainly not walking in the middle of the night on a dirt road. The footsteps were also too light to be the walk of a man.

It could only be her. She had stopped, and turned around to wait for us.

"Is that you?" I thought that it was a stupid question.

"What a stupid question!" she said. "Whom do you want it to be where we are, at this time of the night, and tonight?" she asked.

She read my mind, I thought. I asked, "Did you get the word to everyone?"

"Of course! Do you think that I am not able to do my job?"

"Come on, Michelle! You know that's not what I mean. I just feel responsible for all the boys. Why didn't you pass by my place?

"Too long! I cut through. I was sure to find you somewhere. Don't worry about your boys, as you call them. They will be there, all of them, and nothing will happen to them."

She disconcerted me. I was always wondering about her. I liked her, but she was always slightly aggressive as if to defend herself against I did not know what. Would I like to love her? The question remained unanswered. In any case, she was not encouraging familiarity. Except for the name Michelle, I ignored her real name and had never tried to learn it. Maybe it was Michelle? I knew that the farmers she was living with were not her father and mother. I knew them. They had never called Michelle anything other than Michelle in front of me and had never mentioned any parental link with her. I had neither questioned her about her family, nor about why and how she had ended up there. She would tell me someday if she wanted to. The farm where she lived was some ten minutes away from the hamlet by bicycle. Michelle was very useful. A girl on a bicycle was much less suspicious than a young man.

Father Durand and his cassock was excused. We preferred for him to stay on neutral ground. Fourteen of us were present. Michelle, Marc, and I knew where the field was for the delivery by parachute. A few minutes later, we found Mary and Peter already there.

"We have prepared three small fires with a lot of paper," Mary said. "We have only one flashlight. We have three more but they don't work. Put two of your men with matches at each fire. Take these matchboxes. When we hear the plane, you will light the fires. I don't like it very much, but that's all we can do for tonight. Now, we wait."

A distance of five hundred feet separated the fires that ran in a straight line, and Mary positioned herself at one end with her torch. There is nothing that can be heard more easily than voices in the silence of the night. Silence was the rule, and we waited in silence. The wind was non-existent. Around midnight, we heard the faraway humming of a plane. "The fires," Mary said.

It was our plane. At the extremity of the row of fires, Mary emitted the letter B in Morse with her torch. The plane passed above our heads, and we heard it making a long turn before coming back in alignment with the fires. Immediately, we saw the parachutes opening while the plane flew away. Heavy containers fell on the grass with a dull sound, the parachutes mostly covering them. We had five containers. One could have believed that we had never done anything else in our lives but receive gifts from the sky. In a few minutes, the parachutes were folded and the containers opened.

The parachutes, made of a material resembling strong silk, later became the rage of all the feminine population. After many years of penance in the matter of clothing, such a material was a dream whose second destiny was to be transformed into attractive dresses, skirts, or blouses, or else. The ladies waited, nevertheless, until the departure of the Germans to exhibit their novelties. If the ladies found their joy with the parachutes, the gentlemen who had helped us found theirs when we received a full load of beautiful military leather shoes and American cigarettes instead of ammunition. Mary's only comment was that London was certainly in some kind of a mess.

For now, we had a first supply of Sten submachine guns

that were a total revelation for us, carbines, handguns, and small packages of what looked like gray clay. Mary expressed her satisfaction when she discovered what reminded me of one of my first beloved toys. She was in possession of a small steam engine with a nice copper boiler, a regulator, and a beautiful red wheel with a belt to activate a small black dynamo. It was a wonderful toy.

"Are you dreaming?" Mary's voice brought me back on the grass. "We don't have time for dreaming." I loved Mary for telling me nicely instead of harshly that I should move my ass instead of falling back into infancy.

Everything went fast. The containers ended in the pond. The armament was distributed in three different caches, two in the woods, and one in a dry water tank next to the dependencies of the "castle." Inventory and redistribution would be done later. It would be Marc's job to supervise those jobs and find out for us through Mary the use of those small packages of gray clay.

As soon as everything was taken care of, we sent our men back to their respective homes. Marc, Michelle, and I lingered with Mary and Peter. It was already daylight when we got on our way to return to the village. We were walking quietly when we heard the sound of a plane, the sound of the little German spy plane. It was flying so low that we almost could touch it. The pilot was plainly visible. Better be polite to avoid suspicion. We waved as if he was an old friend, and he waved back to us.

Minus a few minutes, that same guy almost caught us in the act one morning. It was after our second reception. For some reason, the parachutes were not well grouped. When we counted them, one was missing. We searched around rapidly. No parachute. Mary stopped our search. "We will go after the missing one after we have taken care of what we already have," she ordered.

We finally went searching for the missing parachute. Dawn was already there, but no parachute was in sight. Noses up in the woods or down on the grass of the fields, we could not find the parachute. Now the sun showed up above the trees. Each of us had certainly traveled kilometers back and forth. Several of us were back in the meadow where the majestic oak reigned alone.

"Ah! Shit!" one man yelled. "Look at that!"

The majestic oak resembled a gigantic orange mushroom. In the sunlight of a new morning, the parachute displayed the most luminous orange color that one could imagine. It covered the whole top of the tree. Everybody understood. Luckily enough, the other men, Mary, and Peter were joining us. Two men with knives were already in the tree, cutting loose the container that was seized on the ground by all hands available and carried to the woods as if it were weightless. Back to the tree, our "army" pulled the parachute on one side of the tree. The tree was a nice tree that did not object too much at being mistreated. The parachute was soon on the ground. Everybody rushed to the woods.

Just in time. We heard the sound of the engine of the small German spy plane that passed, almost touching the top of the big oak. It was a mania of that pilot to fly at the level of treetops. We buried our noses in the dead leaves. The pilot did not see us. As he never passed twice on the same route the same day – German discipline – we were able to leave separately or in groups of two or three.

We discussed our misadventure afterward. We agreed to try a trick. The three lights were the only way pilots appreciated their altitude for dropping the parachutes, no flying instruments being precise enough at such a low altitude. Why not shorten the distance between the lights to obtain a much more grouped reception?

We did it, reducing by one-third the distance between the lights. That night, the plane after its initial turn to recognize the field, approached us at a lower altitude than usual. The result was a very grouped reception, so grouped that the parachutes had barely enough time to slow down the fall of the containers. I was looking up like everybody else, when I saw that enormous cigar aiming directly at me. I had just enough time to jump aside. The monster fell exactly where I was standing. It went down almost one foot in the ground. Mary had witnessed the whole drama. "OK!" she commented. "If you don't mind, we will go back, next time, to the normal distance between the lights!"

In the meantime, I was still a farmer, farming with my boss, P'tit Louis. Nobody doubts that there is always plenty to do on a farm. I must say that P'tit Louis was happy to see me coming in the morning. All that I did, he did not have to do. And so we were both happy.

That morning, leaving my grandmother's house to go to work and ready to cross the small piazza, I heard "Hello!" and automatically answered "Hello!" My surprise was complete.

She was beautiful. At least it was what I thought when I looked more closely at her. Dressed in black, she had an oval visage, a nose of the right proportion, and nicely drawn lips. Her dark eyes were lighted by some kind of a twinkling flame and dark brown hair rolled over her shoulders. Twenty-five, thirty? Maybe. I had never seen her before. She was standing in front of one of the three houses at the fork of the road. I glanced at the houses. The door of the middle one was open. It had never been open before. She anticipated my question.

"You seem to be surprised to see me here this morning," she said. "You will have to get used to it. I am your neighbor since yesterday. That house belongs to my parents. I hate being bombed and having nothing to eat. For the time being, I'll be much better off here."

Before I could ask her any question, she added that she had not come to the village for many, many years. "Would you help me to find some necessities like food?"

"No problem," I answered. "I work on a farm. I'll be back in less than one hour, and you will have something to eat. What is your name?"

"Suzanne, Suzanne Charpentier."

"Mine is René, René Belleau."

"Well, René, I will wait for you. I have much to do in the house. It has not been open for years, and the only thing you can smell is mold."

I left her and took off in the direction of the farm. After the first excitement of finding on the piazza, early in the morning, coming out of the blue, a nice looking woman, I had to put my thoughts in order. Who was she, and what was her story? One never can tell! I had to find out more about her, and to check, if possible, the information she would give me about herself.

P'tit Louis was happy to see me, as usual. He knew that I had a double life. "Are you here to work?" he asked me with a big smile, always afraid that I would quit. Hearing us talking, Annette came out.

"I need something from you," I told her.

"I knew that you had not come here just to work," Annette said.

My face took a contrite expression.

"It's OK," she said. "Louis cannot join you because I would not be able to do all the work on the farm, but you know that we have always been with you. Now, what can I do for you?"

I explained the reason for my request. But I took the precaution to tell Louis and Annette that, if the woman was coming to their farm to buy some food, they should tell her that I was working on a distant field. "Don't give her any information."

"I am not crazy," Annette said.

"I love you, Annette," I said. "But I don't know that woman, and why she is here. Maybe what she says is the truth, but it costs nothing to be prudent. Maybe she will not try to come here. I will direct her to Marc's grandparents for food. I purposely came here this morning to prove that I am working on a farm."

"How does she look? Annette asked. "Is she nice looking?"

"She is."

"Maybe it's a girl for you."

A few minutes later, I left the farm with a basket of food and walked back to the village. The door of her house was still open. I knocked.

"Come in!" she yelled from the back.

The house had a special disposition. The main room was not at the level of the ground. I had to go down two steps.

"I have never been able to figure out why the floor of that room is lower than the street," she said. "My parents do not know, and nobody gave them an explanation when they bought the house."

I liked Annette even more when I put on the table the content of the basket. There were six eggs, a goat cheese, a piece of bread, four potatoes, two onions, and a bottle of wine. Suzanne insisted on paying but I told her that Annette would be offended by the proposal. For her daily needs, I would introduce her to the farm next door across the road.

"You are OK for today," I said. "I must go to work. See you soon."

"Pass by," she answered. "I will have a glass of wine for you."

"I will."

I returned to the farm, borrowed Annette's bicycle, and went directly to the mission. Marc was there with Mary and Peter, discussing weapons and caches. Marc already knew of the presence of a woman on the piazza. He had not seen her, but his grandmother had. Like all the grandmothers in the country, and certainly in the world, she was immediately aware of something unusual. The three houses in the middle of the fork had been closed since the beginning of the war, and the arrival of a woman in one of them was something definitely unusual.

I gave Mary, Peter, and Marc an exact report on my conversation with the woman whose name was, by the way, Suzanne Charpentier. I also told them about my intention to direct her to Marc's farm for her food.

"Well," I told Marc. "Ask your grandparents for the name of the people who own that house. They certainly remember it. And also, have your grandmother watch her discreetly."

The four of us agreed that Suzanne Charpentier might be "clean," but one never can tell. Mary ordered me to follow up on her invitation for a glass of wine, but to be prudent.

"What am I playing?" I asked. "Do I have the title role in a movie depicting a local female master spy trying to learn my important secrets during a passionate love scene?"

"Don't joke about it," Mary said. "We can never be too prudent. If anything goes wrong, don't hesitate. I am going to give you a very small revolver, since you don't have one. This one is flat, and three and a half inches long. Carry it in your pocket when you visit her. I am not kidding. I don't believe that I am overdoing it. She may be a genuine little Frenchwoman; she may, as well, be working for the Germans. There are some eyes and ears that are not friendly around here, but we have a tendency to relax and feel secure. Watch out, René, because it's your turn to play the game. Like in the movies, as you said."

I had to follow my routine and, I came back around six o'clock. Before going to my grandmother's house, I stopped at Marc's farm.

"Their name was Charpentier," his grandmother told me. "That proves nothing," I thought to myself. "I am sure that there is a René Belleau somewhere who does not know that a counterfeited document gave him a twin brother three years older than he is."

"But," Marc's grandmother added, "I don't remember seeing a young girl in that house."

Her door was open. I did not stop and went straight to my grandmother. I explained to her that I had to go out to pay a visit to the woman on the piazza. I left my grandmother and her ironic smile, to go and knocked at the open door.

"Come in, and sit down!"

There was a waxed table in the middle of the room with four straw chairs, a chimney whose aperture was closed by a stove as it was at my grandmother's house, a nice cup-board, and, surprisingly, a small library with books on the shelves. "Only classical titles," she said, as I looked at them. "That's my father. He always needs some books around him. But let's drink to our meeting. Don't tell me that you were born here and are a real farm worker," she said with a smile. "The first thing you did was to look at the books. You betrayed yourself, but I won't betray you. It's a secret between you and me."

I almost bit my tongue. I had a lot to learn if I wanted to make a career in the spying business. She was way ahead of me. I hated the pistol in my pocket. I gave her the best image I could of a boy who had preferred to quit Paris where life was very difficult and food scarce, and come to live with his grandmother. She had done the same, and she certainly understood me.

She put a hand on mine. Her hand was soft and warm. I liked it.

"And I am sure that you are just a little older that you pretend," she said with a smile. "You can tell me, or do you want me to guess."

I hated Mary. I knew that I was, by accident, the only person in position to play the game with that woman, but I was uneasy. That woman was ahead of me. She had a nice smile and was still beautiful, according to my judgment of the moment. She represented the perfect temptation. I could not figure out if she was a cat playing with a stupid mouse, or if she was a pure dove taking pleasure at teasing me.

We had one glass of wine and, then, a second. She kissed me on the cheek and told me to go back home. "Come back tomorrow," she said.

"I will! I will bring a bottle of wine."

The following evening, I knocked at her open door, a bottle of wine in my hands, and the small pistol in my pocket with my handkerchief on top of it to round its angles. We sat, close to each other at a corner of the table. We spoke mostly of literature and music during the first glass of wine.

"And so, you pretend that you are a farm boy," she said while I was pouring a second glass of wine.

"I do not pretend anything anymore." I put my hand on hers. She did not pull her hand away. I had done much thinking during the night to improve my career as a spy. "I do not pretend anymore," I repeated, "but tell me what is true and is not true in your own story. It's your turn."

It took her a third glass of wine to tell me again the same story that she had already given me. We remained silent for a while until she said, "It's time for you to go home." We got up. Maybe with wine helping, I took her in my arms. She did not resist, and I kissed her when she offered her lips.

My experience with women was naught. In fact, beside my time with my family, which was not a time for libertinage even when on the beaches in summer, I had spent most of my life in one-sex schools and colleges. La Sainte Beaume where nobody was available had not been a ground for experimentation, even less the Chantiers de Jeunesse. I was sure that if occasions had presented themselves in the past, I had not taken advantage of them by natural timidity reinforced by the good principles imprinted in my conscience by my Christian education.

But, all of a sudden, the tie was loosing up. I was holding in my arms a more or less consenting woman, practically for the first time, someone that my arms and hands around her identified as female. When she felt that I was becoming more pressing, she stepped back. "Not tonight," she said. "In a few days." She woke me up with those words. It was about time. I had to improve on my behavior as a spy and not let my repressed sexual instincts take over my mind.

The following evening, I knocked at her door that was not closed. The small pistol was not in my pocket. I could not stand it, and she could discover it. A bottle of wine was in my hands.

"Come in and sit down!"

We were at our third glass when she said, "René, I know that you do not know what to think about me. I believe that I know you well enough now to trust you. I also guess that you have a lot of friends around. The truth is that I am here with a purpose."

"Does that house belong to your parents?" I asked.

"To a friend."

"You lied to me."

"Yes, I did, but you will understand why. I am here with a job to do. Don't interrupt me. I am an envoy from London in charge of organizing the resistance in this area, and provide it with armaments. This is where you can come in and help me, darling."

I thought that she was a damned liar. I did not say a word while she went on, "We have a logistical support. I already have a location accepted by London for the dropping by plane of the weapons we need. Tomorrow, if you agree, I will show you the place. It's not too far away. We can walk."

"May I ask you a few questions?"

"No, darling, you cannot. I will tell you nothing, at least for now. If we work together, you will learn more."

"In that case, can I kiss you?"

I was obliged to play the game. The first thing to do was to rush to tell Mary, this very night, the latest and important development of the story. It was not difficult to enjoy kissing the so-called Suzanne, even if she was a damned liar, and eventually a very dangerous woman. All of a sudden I remembered drawings of "Dance Macabre" of the Middle Ages, where death had the visage of a woman. I was not sure, yet. Only the visit to the site would determine the final truth, but I figured out the truth. If the truth was what I figured out, it was I who represented death, and my kiss was a kiss of death because we would act before she could. A great pity for her invaded my mind. I kissed her again.

"Tomorrow." she said. "Tomorrow morning we will go to the space that I want to show you. Then, after that, you will go to work. I will wait for you in the evening. It's my turn for the bottle of wine." She looked at me and smiled. I could have sworn that it was the smile of an angel. "You may stay tomorrow night, if you wish."

I crossed the little piazza, full of confused sentiments. I took the time to tell the whole story to my grandmother, sure that she would make some valuable comments. I also wanted to let the light on for a while in the main room, so that if Suzanne watched the house, she would believe that, after a while, I went to bed and turned off the light. Actually, the only comment of my grandmother was that I had to do what I had to do. "I saw her," she said. "Yes, she is nice looking, but if she is what you say, she a nice-looking snake that will kill you all if you don't get rid of her. How? I don't know. That's your business." My grandmother had not used the word beautiful. As to the rest of her comments, I thought that she had, perhaps, read too many spy stories, but she was right.

I turned off the light, opened the window of my bedroom, jumped outside, passed behind the church, and took off across the fields in the direction of the mission. Forty minutes later, I was telling Mary the whole story. First, her eyes opened wide. She looked at me as if she did not believe the London story. But, then, with her cool British attitude back, she declared that two British missions would never overstep each other in the same area. That was impossible. She would ask London for confirmation, but she was already sure that the whole affair was a hoax.

"You know what that means?" she added.

"She works for the Germans," I said. "She supposes that I am some kind of a leader. That's because of the books. She will tell me tomorrow when I will have to bring my troop to the drop place so that our men and I will be dead or prisoners."

"Did you make love with her?"

Now I wanted to appear like a man with some experience of women. I answered with a slight tone of negligence in my voice, wondering if Mary would buy it, "I told you no. Love is for tomorrow night."

"That will make it easier for you. No sentiments involved. This is what I suggest."

The next morning at seven, Suzanne and I left the village. She seemed to know perfectly well where she was going. It confirmed definitively our suspicion that her whole plot was set up before she came to the village. Perhaps she knew of the existence of the real British mission and intended to capture its members by the same token. Several scenarios were running full speed in my head while I was looking at her walking at my side.

She was leading me to our own territory. I guessed that her drop space was also ours. It was the only sensible space available in the area for that type of operation, and she could not present me with a poor location.

"Here it is," she said showing me the field that I knew so well. "Day after tomorrow, during the night, at exactly one in the morning, a plane will drop what we need to organize a solid network of resistance. I am sure that you have enough friends to help me take care of the material. We will have to hide it in a place that I will indicate to you."

"How many men do you need?"

"The more you have with you, the easier and faster it will be done. Do you have twenty men to carry the merchandise?"

"I do," I answered. "Even a little more. I can guarantee you that they will be here."

"I knew that you were the man I needed," she said.

"How did you know that?"

"Feminine intuition. You are too cultured and intelligent, not to be the leader here," she said flattering me. "You are ready for action, and I provide you with action. Let's go back to the village."

I left her when I had to turn and take the path to P'tit Louis's farm.

"See you tonight," I said.

"I will wait for you with a bottle of wine."

From the farm, I rushed to the mission where Mary was waiting for me with impatience.

"No such a thing," Mary declared. "The whole thing is what we said, a German hoax. She is a very dangerous woman."

I told Mary everything without forgetting a detail.

"We must act fast," Mary concluded. "We must arrest her and play dead with the Germans. We ignore how she communicates with her boss. She certainly does not have a compromising radio transmitter at home. Perhaps the telephone booth at the "village at the bridge?" It's enough. Does she have a bicycle? It is probable that if they do not hear from her tomorrow, they will cancel." Otherwise, they will come to surround you and will find out that nobody will show up, including their super agent. She will have disappeared. They will never know if she was a truthful agent or if she double-crossed them. No! They will wait for confirmation tomorrow, and they will not come."

Mary made a short pause. "Now, mon petit René," she said, "you know what you have to do. You are the only one frequenting that young person, the only one to whom she will open her door if her door were closed. You need two or three men with you. She may resist. Be very prudent. Much depends on you! Any decision you make, I will support. But be extremely prudent."

I found Marc at his grandparents' farm. I told him straight that we had a dirty job to do. "I knew that you visited her," Marc said. "You remember that you told my grand-mother to watch her. She is a nice-looking girl, and I thought you were just trying to go to bed with her. You never told me anything else."

"Yes, she is a nice looking girl," I said, "but one who is ready to send you to hell. Get Eugene! We meet at the rectory at six. I'll be obliged to tell the story to Father Durand. In any case, he will learn it. Earlier or later makes no difference."

Eugene and Marc were behind me when I knocked at her door. When she answered, "Come in!," she was seated at the table. They literally jumped on her, pushing me aside. She did not seem to understand what was happening. Marc and Eugene were strong men. Before she could react, they applied their strength on her arms and shoulders to keep her on her chair. First, she tried to liberate herself, but finding it useless, she did not move anymore. She looked at me with Interrogative eyes. "René!" she said, " say something! What does this mean?"

She was still beautiful, but her charm had a reverse effect on me.

"You know perfectly well what this means," I said. "You work for the Germans, and you took me for an idiot. You imagined that you were going to destroy our network of resistance.
You were even ready to make love with me, darling, to achieve your goal. With your angel face, you were ready to kill every one of us, including me. Why not in your bed after love?"

My own words were making me angry. A visible change transformed her visage. Her previous reflex of snared animal fighting for freedom had made place to an expression of defiance and contempt. I grasped the change. Inside her was a devil.

"You are not a woman!" I almost screamed, guessing, "You are a Gestapo member."

"And proud to be," she screamed back. "I am German. I

speak French as well as you do because I had all my schooling in France. I am a Sorbonne graduate."

I was completely bewildered. Was that woman for real? But before I could put things in order in my mind, and relate Sorbonne and Nazi fanaticism, I had to make my move. Marc and Eugene were looking at me.

"Come with us!" I told her gently. "Come with us, there is still time. They will never find you. Tell me what you know about us. How do you know about London?"

"Never! You hear me, never! You are all going to die, anyway. We will crush you like vermin!"

I extended my hand in Marc's direction and he put his .45 in it. I armed it and approached Suzanne's forehead with its barrel. I hoped that I would wake up at the end a bad dream, but it was not a dream. I was facing a madwoman.

"Suzanne...!" I started.

"Marika!" she interrupted me.

"Marika, if you wish.... If you want to stay alive, tell me what you know about us. I promise you that we will treat you as a war prisoner if you tell me everything you know."

"I swore my allegiance to Adolph Hitler, not to you."

She spat in my direction. I could not believe it. She tried violently to get rid of the boys, but after useless moves, she remained immobile. The barrel of the gun came back to her forehead.

"Marika, please!" I shouted.

"Never! Never! Never!" she screamed. "Go to hell!"

I pulled the trigger. It made a round hole in her forehead and the back of her head exploded. Marc and Eugene had not moved. They were as surprised as I was by the ending of that tragedy. They finally stepped back. Marika remained seated as she was.

"She would have killed us with no pity," Marc said. "I believe that I would not have waited as long as you did before pulling the trigger. She already knew too much. We would have never been able to drag her or to carry her to the mission. The house has a backyard, a small garden. Let's bury her there for now. Eugene and I will dig the hole. I cannot ask my grandparents to bury her on their farm. My grandmother would never stop thinking about that, and I don't want her to get sick because of that woman. We have nowhere else to bury her than here, and she deserves nothing more than to be buried like a dog. Father Durand will pray for her soul if he wants."

We carried Marika's body to the garden where we discovered a bicycle. Mary was right. She needed no more than a bicycle to go to the telephone booth. With no news from her, the Germans would cancel their operation. I did not know about Marc and Eugene, but I walked in a sort of vertigo. I, the artist, supposed to devote my life to beauty, had killed with my own hands a human being. Worse, I had killed a woman.

"Yes," I said aloud, "but the Germans know that she was here. Let's only hope that they won't come. They would find out that we killed her. On the other hand, we cannot clean that room, especially the plaster on the wall. We have to take the risk."

"Go back home," Marc said. "Eugene and I will finish the job. Don't worry."

I was nervously exhausted, but I still had to be the leader. "Thank you, both of you," I said. "It will change nothing if I see Mary tonight. I will go and see her in the morning."

My grandmother was not in bed. She asked no question when she saw me coming in. She waited for me to talk. I told her everything. She manifested no surprise.

"My boy," she finally said, "you did what you had to do. It was your duty. Evil cannot triumph forever."

Knowing my grandmother, it was my turn not to be surprised by her words. She was the reverse of a defeatist and had some iron running in her veins. I am sure that she could have pulled the trigger herself. Nonetheless, it was good to receive family approval for the liquidation of a female spy.

"René," my grandmother added, "don't let that story upset you. I understand that you are shocked. You are still very young, and it is not the type of experience that a boy of your age should have. I would prefer to see you dancing with a nice girl, but it is war. And war is cruel, but you fight for a just cause. You must go on, whatever happens."

I believed that Marika's drama would keep me awake, but I slept. Awaking in the morning, images of the evening jostled in my mind. For a few seconds, I thought of myself as a psychopathic killer going to bed and sleeping like a baby after murdering a woman. Luckily enough, reality was slightly different.

I gave Mary all the details. "She made me so mad, she was so evil that I killed her," I said. "I did not know what to do. In any case, we would have been unable to bring that fury here. We buried her in the backyard of the house, like a dog. We must thank Marc and Eugene for that. It may create a future problem when the owners come back, but we had no other solution. We also left the room as is. It would have been impossible for us to clean up the mess. We had no way to do it, and I did not want to do it. She would have killed you, me, all our men with no pity. She was a fanatic. How is it possible that she was such a fanatic? What has Hitler done to them? I don't understand. And I killed her."

Mary waited a minute before talking. "Listen, René," she finally said, "if you had not killed her, we would have. What else could have we done? We do not even have a place to keep such a rabid animal, and she would always try to escape. As you said, she would have killed all of us. She deserved her death. That's part of war, René. Don't feel guilty. She would have been pleased to kill you, even after making love with you. This affair means that we must be more prudent than ever. 'They' will try by all means to destroy us because they know that we exist. To what extent we exist is what they don't know. Not only did you do right, René, but we must thank you for your determination. It was an act of courage for an artist. Let's only hope that the Germans will not come!"

Mary seemed to lose herself in her thoughts. Then she added, "You were lucky. Let me tell you why. Imagine... just imagine for an instant, that we had not been here, the mission, which was your only means to verify her tale. You were eager to do something, to create a Resistance group. That woman promised you that she was going to help you because she comes from London, and you have no reason to question what she tells you. It seems so authentic. She would have made love with you to prove to you that she was sincere. That's part of her job. You were a little fly in her cobweb. Tell me honestly! What would have you done? You had many chances to succumb to her sex appeal and London appeal, and to be dead or tortured to death by now, with her watching."

Mary's words were painful. Superman could not have resisted the call of the siren and the London coloring of her tale. In other words, my career would have ended abruptly, emptied of my substance in the bed of a spider, and tortured in the jails of the Gestapo. As Mary said, I had been lucky.

On the other hand, Mary's reassuring words put some balm on my wounded mind, but I doubted that I would ever forget killing a woman at point blank, even if my action were more than justified, even if I saved my own life, and my friends' lives. Fortunately, I had not made love with her. I could not imagine what my feelings would have been if I had killed her after making love with her. I was not a professional spy utilizing that type of weapon. Perhaps I was too innocent or unwilling to confront the realities of some aspects of war. I still wanted to preserve a little blue flower in my heart. I found it very hard to do, at least at that moment.

The Germans never came to inquire about the disappearance of their agent Marika. Why they did not will remain a mystery. I even considered the crazy hypothesis that she was not a German agent but some kind of schizophrenic woman playing a dangerous game to its limit, guessing that I would never pull the trigger. But that hypothesis raised even more questions. I will never know.

When I met Michelle two days later, none of us made the slightest allusion to the German drama. I could not guess if she knew what went on. In any case, she acted as if she knew nothing. I was still working at P'tit Louis farm, and P'tit Louis was very pleased with my work. I had never worked so hard. That was part of my anti-killer therapy. "What shall I do when you will no longer be here?" he asked me. I answered him that he would do as he did before my arrival. I supposed that he was considering the amount of work that I was doing and that he would have to do. He was also certainly considering the fact that he would be obliged to pay a conscientious helper more than a dinner and a few things for his grandmother.

Late in the evening of June fifth, I came back as usual to sleep at my grandmother's house. P'tit Louis, Annette, and I had lingered after dinner. I was tired and it was late. I fell asleep almost immediately. Two hours later, someone knocked violently on the door. A voice called from outside. "It's Father Durand! Open up! Open up! Quick!"

My grandmother was already at the door. Father Durand was in a high state of excitement. "John let his beard grow!" he almost screamed. "John let his beard grow! You know what it means?"

"I know. It's for tonight. I must see Mary first thing in the morning. There is not much that we can do right now."

My grandmother was looking at both of us with bewilderment.

"They land today, tonight perhaps," I told her. "This is it! They land! It means that we have to fight, and we are ready for it!"

It was action, at last. It was all I had waited for since La Sainte Beaume. Where was Christian at that minute? I was becoming sentimental at the wrong moment. There was great excitement at the mission in the early morning. We were now really at war. We would have to help the Allies by all means at our disposal.

We had a complete arsenal for one hundred people: Sten submachine guns, M1 Carbines, P45 enormous revolvers, plastic explosives, and detonators. It was more than we needed for the twelve warriors that we were. In fact, we were a little short in effective force to carry on our war against Germany. But that was not enough to discourage us.

"That's it," Mary said. "You were, we were all waiting for this day. Now, let's be practical. From now on," she said addressing me, "you and your men stay nearby. This is what we are going to do. You know that past the guardhouse and the "castle," let's call it castle, there are what they call the dependencies with stables for horses and a barn. We are going to see the landlord and tell him that we requisition the dependencies. That's where you will stay with your men, at least momentarily."

The "castle" was not really a castle but a nice, vast, two-story square house built with white stones that gave it an aspect of a castle. Compared to the farmhouses of the area, or even the houses of the "village at the bridge," it was effectively a castle. An old gentleman and his wife with an air of old country nobility fitting the house received Mary, Peter, Marc, and me.

The secret had been so well kept that they ignored the presence of the mission in their guardhouse. They had no servants and rarely went out of their house. The guard I had met when I came in for the first time provided them with their needs. In their minds, we became instantly trespassers and intruders. We could feel their prime hostility.

Mary was very polite. They slightly relaxed, but we perceived their lack of enthusiasm for the presence of the Resistance on their domain. I did not know if it were because of the label "Resistance," or simply because of the presence of so many people on their property. They were defenders, not of the Germans, but of Marshal Pétain. The old gentleman had fought under Pétain during World War One. For him, the Marshal was still the hero of Verdun.

We told them that we had the greatest respect for the Marshal, but, as sorry as we could be, his days were over. In any case, we had a job to do. We had to help the Allied. In order to do our job, we had to stay on their property and occupy the dependencies for the time being.

"I believe I cannot oppose your action," the old gentleman said.

"To be honest with you, no!" Mary answered. "But we represent a danger for you. I suggest that you leave your house for the time that we are here. We can help you. The Germans...."

"Never!" interrupted the old gentleman. "Never! Here we live, and here we stay."

"As you wish. I only gave you my advice."

And thus, we took possession of the dependencies that had nothing remarkable except that they were made out of red bricks, the timber was of good quality, and there was no mess around or inside. No horses lived in the stalls that were very clean. For the boys who wanted to sleep inside, their mattress would be of concrete, but so what? The option of sleeping on a bed of leaves in the woods was available.

The first surprise happened at noon. I was up the stairs of the guardhouse, discussing accommodations and strategy – if there were one – with Mary and Peter, when we saw three young men at the gate "Let me see what they want," I said. I rushed down the stairs.

"We want to join," they declared.

"Join what?"

"Your group."

It was of no use to ask, "Which group?" Instead, I asked them how they knew of the existence of a "group."

"Arabian telephone," one of them answered.

Arabian telephone is a French expression coined when France took over North Africa during its colonial expansion. It is the telephone without wires, the word of mouth traveling long distances and fast.

"And if I ask you who gave you the information, or where the information comes from, you will tell me that you don't know."

"Correct!"

I gave up. I accompanied them to our quarters in the dependencies. I put them in Marc's hands. "Eh, Marc!" I said. "You are the boss here. They are all yours."

I did not see much of Michelle during those days that became so hectic. Five days later, we were one hundred in the dependencies. They were coming from all over and from we did not know where. All guns had been removed from storage and distributed. Marc had learned how to use the

62

gray clay for sculpture. It was nothing other than an explosive. No professional soldier who could have helped with the weapons knocked at the gate, but a professional cook did. Our new chef was immediately put in charge of the important matter of meals. He found enough tables and material in the dependencies to install two large tables in front of the stables.

A positive result of the D-Day was that the small spy plane was no longer flying above our heads, at least during the following days. Its pilot would have immediately spotted the movement in the dependencies. A negative aspect of our sudden population explosion was that the meals were rapidly becoming a nightmare. We had to provide all those stomachs with food. Marc and Eugene, and the members of our first group, were the only ones who knew the farms where we could find food, but it was creating constant traffic on the roads. In the dependencies was a "Citroën Traction Avant" that Marc had discovered without saying where. "In case," he had declared. "In case" was on its way to becoming a habit by the necessity.

"I don't like it," I told Mary. "There is no possibility to verify where those men come from and who they are. If they can find us so easily, so can the Germans. Any of those guys could be a spy. Food becomes a bigger problem daily, and makes our presence more visible. We should move out of here for a few days."

Mary agreed with me. "I will move our radioman no later than today. He is our most precious man, and he has been here long enough. The Germans would finally discover him by triangulation. We have a farm where he will be secure for now. That's where we will go ourselves. I'll tell you where it is. You should move tomorrow. See with Marc where you can go and let me know."

Marc shared my fears. He thought that it was wise to

move our "army" out of the dependencies. But it was more difficult to move one hundred men than twelve, and there were not that many places where we could go. The most convenient was a small wood six kilometers away. It was not an ideal solution. The wood was too small to be secure, but we had no ideal solution at our disposal. We had to move at night if we did not want to expose our moving column to enemy eyes that could be anywhere during the day. Every man would carry a gun and its ammunition, even though most of them did not know how to use a gun. We would move the next night. We would leave the Citroën hidden in the barn. Marc would pick it up later to go shopping. If nothing happened, we could always come back to the dependencies.

We woke up at dawn. Our chef had already prepared a breakfast for all and placed the food on the tables. The day promised to be a nice, sunny day of early June. I was ready to pick up something to eat when we heard a strangled "couac" followed by another "couac." "Damn it! The trumpet!" Marc screamed, "Alert! Pick up your guns!"

There was no mistake. Marc had organized a watchman's post, just out of the woods in front of the guardhouse. On top of a ladder supported by the branch of a tall tree, the view extended over a kilometer of road. The watchman had a trumpet that he was supposed to blow if some danger appeared.

At that I screamed to Marc, "Let's take the car! We'll go faster to see what's happening."

Marc and I jumped in the car. Two men jumped in the car behind us, on the back seat. Marc pushed the gas pedal to the floor on the small alley leading to the castle that we passed. All of a sudden, I put my hand on Marc's arm. "Slow down!" I commanded. One second later, I commanded again with a harsh voice, "Turn left!" and another second later, "Stop, and get out!"

Slowing down and turning left were my pure instinct. Window open, I had not been able to hear any other noise than the car running full speed. When it slowed down, I heard no other noise than the car running slowly, but the trumpet had told us one thing: the Germans were here. What about the mission and the trumpeter? I did not know. What I knew was that we could not offer any resistance to the Germans because we were absolutely unprepared for it. We were in no condition to fight a well-organized and well-armed enemy.

No noise other than the car could mean that we were throwing ourselves in the lion's open mouth. The Germans might already be in the woods. At my order, Marc automatically turned left in the middle of the trees for there was no road on the left. Without asking any question, he jumped out of the car. The men in the back did alike. I opened my door on the side facing the gate visible a little further and did the same. The trees were poorly hiding German uniforms. A shower of bullets made holes in the car, missing me. It was not my day to die. I ran, and ran so fast that I teamed again with Marc within a few seconds. We kept on running until we were out of the reach of the German guns.

I did not care about Mary and Peter. They were "old enough" to survive by themselves if the Germans had not caught them. I must confess that I did not think at all about the castle and its two inhabitants. I was worried about our "army." The problem was to find our men who were certainly dispersed in the woods, regroup them if possible, and see how we could deal with the Germans.

One hour later, we were fifty-five on the road at the extremity of the woods. In order to be more precise, let's say that the "castle" was at the north edge of the woods, and that we were actually at the southern extremity of the woods. Most of the men had guns that they had grabbed when they heard the alarm and had not abandoned them while flying into the woods. That was good. It proved that they had not completely panicked.

The Germans were now two kilometers away. I saw a young man with a carbine and a pistol. I asked him to give me his pistol. Marc and I had jumped into the car without weapons. Now I was armed. I doubted that I could do much against a German machine gun if I had to face one, but in front of all those young people looking at me with anxiety, I had to act like a chief.

With that ridiculous weapon in my hand, I started walking north in the ditch on the side of the road in the direction of the Germans. The two kilometers seemed to be two hundred. The road made several curves, and at each one of those curves, I was wondering if I were not going to find myself nose to nose with a German, but nothing happened until we reached the north end of the woods.

A German truck stood in the middle of the road, some two thousand feet away. Several other trucks were visible behind it, but the first truck had a machine gun on the roof of its cab, and the gunner thought that it was intelligent to shoot at us.

He aimed too high and only the leaves of the trees suffered. It was a warning. There was nothing we could do with Stens and carbines against machine guns.

None of us had even fired a Sten. Peter had given a course on Stens the previous day. "They are wonderful weapons," he said, with one in his hands. "However they have a few problems. As you can see, they look cheap... because they are cheap. Every blacksmith in England manufactures them. If you look close, they look unfinished and they are unfinished. Look where the trigger mechanism is welded onto the receiver. See the butt? It looks as if it was a closet hanger, but it is the easiest weapon to dismantle. I'll show you. For all those reasons, two Stens will not necessarily have the same characteristics, meaning that they will not fire exactly in the same way. But that is of almost no importance for the other reason that you cannot really aim at one target and shoot one bullet. You miss. I'll show you. Even if you shoot your whole magazine you miss again because, as soon as you pull the trigger, the machine goes up at a slant. If you want to kill your man, you must start shooting three or four feet aside of him and very low. You have the best chance to get him from the waist up.

"A wise precaution is to load only 30 rounds instead of the possible 32. Thus, there is less strain exercised on the magazine's weak spring. It means that your Sten will have fewer occasions for jamming, which is also one of its characteristics. And it always jams at a critical moment. Never leave a bullet engaged. Take the magazine off if you are not in action. You are all aware of what happened the other day. We don't need to kill our own because that gun goes off if you bump it against something. It is nevertheless a weapon very useful in close combat situation if you use it well. Unfortunately, we do not have ammunition to train you. You will have to use the best of your judgment after what I have told you."

"What happened the other day" marked one of the worst episodes in what my life had been, so far, even after the Marika drama. Early in the morning, the three of them, father, mother, and son appeared at the gate. They asked for the chief or the commander of the group. I went to meet them. The son was a nice-looking young man, tall, brown hair, brown eyes, the look of a student and not of a farm boy. The parents were certainly not farmers. I did not wish to know.

"Our son wants absolutely to join you," the father told me. "He is very young..."

"I'll be eighteen this year...."

"Our son is very young," the father continued. "We have tried to dissuade him but to no avail. We prefer to give him to you rather than see him flying away without our consent. So, here we are and here is our son Paul."

"I leave him in your care," the mother said. "We are not far away, only eight kilometers in the second village south, the last house on Main Street. He can always come back, if he wants. But we are also afraid of the Germans. He is just old enough to be sent to Germany."

"I'll take care of him. I promise," I said.

They say goodbye to one another, and the parents left as silently as they had come. They were now two instead of three passing the gate. They did not turn their heads. I accompanied Paul to the dependencies, and presented him to Marc, telling Marc that Paul's parents had accompanied him. I left them to go back to the guardhouse where I still had a lot of business to discuss with Mary. How to organize all those men, how to give them some discipline? How to feed them? How this? How that? We also had to create a group specializing in the use of explosives, and so on. I was still there two hours later. I was ready to leave when we heard the characteristic sound of a Sten. I literally jumped down the staircase and ran to the dependencies.

From a distance, I could see that a big commotion had taken place. On the side of the building were several benches made of concrete. A compact group of men surrounded one of them. "Let me pass!" I yelled. The group opened in front of me. Paul was on the bench, his head reversed on the back of the bench, immobile, his waist full of blood, his shirt torn apart on both sides of his body. Marc was there. He looked at me and only said, "He is dead."

I felt struck by lightning. I could not realize that this nice boy was dead two hours after his mother had left him in my care. I could not imagine that I, and nobody else, would have to tell his mother that her son had joined us just in time to meet his death. I was dumfounded.

"What happened?" I asked.

Absolutely frantic, the owner of the Sten was unable to talk. "I saw the whole thing," a young man said. "We were having something to eat and, you know, we wanted to sit. Those two went to sit on the bench. They were already seated when Raymond's Sten slipped down from his shoulder and fell on the bench. When it knocked the bench, the whole volley went off and hit Paul."

The so-called Raymond was going mad. He was yelling, "I killed him! I killed him!" The Sten was on the ground. He grabbed it suddenly and crashed it on the bench with all his strength. Everyone seemed paralyzed and did not move when he ploughed through our group and started running. We never saw him afterward.

Paul's body was almost cut in two parts. His organs were reduced into a red aggregate. I told Marc to get a plank to put him on for now, and later carry him to his parents. I had to tell the mission what had happened. I also needed two bed sheets, one to tie around Paul's waist to keep his body in one piece, and one to envelop him in a shroud on the plank.

"Tonight, " I told Marc, "we will have to carry him back to his parents. We cannot bury him here. Don't say a word. I feel so miserable that I almost wish I were dead in his place. I cannot imagine his parents' reaction. We had him for two hours, Marc, only two hours, and in my care! Perhaps those machine guns will help us to win the war but they are damned pieces of shit! And we had better watch out so that they do not kill all our men."

Mary and Peter came down to the dependencies. They were sincerely sorry. Mary looked annoyed and miserable. You had to have a solid heart to move and tie a folded bed sheet around Paul's body. Mary and Peter helped. The wounds were horrific to look at, and there was blood all over. We felt better after the first turn of the sheet around Paul's waist. We made two turns. Marc had nailed two transversal pieces of wood under the plank to serve as handles. We wrapped Paul on the plank in the second bed sheet.

Carrying Paul through the woods at night to avoid the road was not easy. After a long detour around the first village, it took us three hours to reach the back of the last house in Main Street of the second village. Main Street was the road. There was no other way for me than coming to the front door. I knocked discreetly but insistently. The door opened after a while, showing the face of Paul's mother in the light of an oil lamp.

"Oh, my God!" she said, recognizing me. "Please. Come in! Don't raise your voice. My husband is sleeping."

Before I could speak, she asked, softly, "It's Paul? What's wrong? What happened to Paul?" Was it her maternal instinct or was it written on my face? I don't know. She only asked again, softly, "He is dead, isn't it?"

I inclined my head. I was expecting some violent reaction from her but she controlled herself completely. She remained silent, eyes closed, her jointed hands on her mouth as if she was praying.

"God gives, God takes!" she said. "He absolutely insisted on joining you. I had a premonition. He walked to his death like an angel. I am almost not surprised. He had such an innocent soul."

Tears came to my eyes. I was astonished by her simple dignity and calm courage.

"Where is my boy?" she asked. "Tell me briefly what happened before I wake up my husband." I told her how the drama had happened. I did not hide the fact that the wounds were not nice to look at.

"He is my son," she answered me. "He is the blood of my blood, and I can put my hands in his blood. I can take my bloody son in my arms. A mother can do that. Tell that boy who killed my son that he should not carry his death on his conscience. He may come here and visit us. My pain and my husband's pain are our concern. Whatever happened is not your fault. You are no more responsible for his death than you are responsible for the war. It is the war that took my son, not you. I will manage to have Paul buried in such a way that nobody will know the truth, and you will have no problems because of that. The Germans, I mean. Now, tell your men to bring him in. There is a door in the backyard. I am going to wake up my husband, but I want you to be gone before I do it."

I took and kissed her hand. "Go, now," she said.

The gunman fired again two or three times at random, scorching the leaves around us. The result of the first volley had been that half of us crashed into the woods on the right, and half, including me, on the left where the woods ended in open fields. On that side, we had a small declivity covered by a few trees and bushes to protect us. They did not have a declivity on the right side but the bushes were thick and the trees abundant. Eugene and his men disappeared but, I was sure, without retreating.

It was impossible for one of the groups to cross the road to regroup without being spotted by the gunner. There was only one thing I could do: tell Eugene and his men to retreat and go down the hill to a sheep stable located at the southern extremity of the woods. It would constitute our meeting place. But in order to tell that to Eugene, I had to cross the road.

I had two options, crawling or walking. I thought that crawling, if spotted, would be very suspicious and, hence, dangerous. Walking was a question of luck. There were three possibilities: the gunman was busy at something else or not looking in my direction, or he would not immediately make the distinction between me and one of his colleagues. Or he would make the distinction, fire, and miss. I took "my courage in my hands," as the French say. I crossed the road, walking but not running, my heart pounding, and expecting to be killed.

Nothing happened; no bullets flew around me. On the other side were Eugene and twenty or more men. "Listen, Eugene," I told him, "retreat to the sheep stable. You know where it is. Wait for us over there as long as we don't show up. If you are in danger, you have the woods, but stay there; otherwise we will lose each other. I swear to you that we'll be back. We are going to try something. I don't know what, but you would be of no help and you cannot cross the road with your group. We just can try a small diversion to sting the Germans to let them know that they did not get us. That's all we can do at the moment. We are more than we need for that. I am going to keep a dozen men and send the others down the hill to join you at the sheep place. I suppose that the Germans did not penetrate very far into the woods.

They did not even use this road to see what's going on in the woods. They certainly went to the castle and the dependencies because of the alley. But all that is supposition."

I addressed the men, "Eugene is your chief. You do exactly what he tells you to do. We will regroup at night. We lost a battle; we did not lose the war. Who said that before me? You will leave as soon as I am on the other side. If you do it calmly without noise, the Germans will not even know that you were here. See you later."

I had to cross the road again. Again I took my courage in my hands, as the French say, and crossed. The machine gun remained silent for an unknown reason.

"Not very brilliant our day, so far," I told Marc. Then I whispered, addressing all the men, "Half of you will leave to join the other guys at the bottom of the hill, and wait for us. I want ten guys to make a diversion. Marc and I agree that we should try to reach the small grove that stands between here and the river, just where the road goes down again toward the bridge of the village, and see if we can do something against the Germans passing back and forth."

All the men were on their bellies, watching in the direction of the machine gun. "I will pick one of you out of two," I said. I pointed my finger. "One, three, five...." I stopped after selecting ten men. Adding Marc and me, we were a dozen. Twelve, a dozen, always seems to be the right number, the magic number, the number that comes automatically to mind. Marc designated a leader who knew where to go and put him in charge of those who were leaving.

As soon as we moved on after their departure, we were no longer in the woods but in open fields, and we had to make a long detour to avoid being marked by the machine-gun. From afar, the trucks were now visible as a file. "There are not so many trucks," I told Marc. "They are not an army."

We reached the grove. From that position, we could see a portion of the road going down in the direction of the river. We neglected to check the view on the right for an incredible reason, one of those facts that you do not believe, even if they happen in front of you. A man and two women were promenading on the road, right in front of us, as if they had been pleasuring in a quiet public park with all the Germans peacefully at home in faraway Germany. It was really an incredible vision. The man, in his forties, had his arms around the backs of the women and his hands on their waists. He was certainly telling them something very funny for they were roaring with laughter. Marc and I jumped on the road. "Get the hell out of here!" Marc shouted. "Or stay here if you want to die!" Their surprise turned into terror when they saw our weapons. I had borrowed a carbine from one of the men that we had sent to the sheep stable.

They were hardly out of our sight when we heard a motorcycle coming from the bridge. It had a sidecar, and was running at very moderate speed. We formed an almost perfect line of fire with me as last man on the left of that line. We all fired when the sidecar passed in front of us. I fired once, but the carbine refused to fire twice. The sidecar stopped abruptly just after it passed in front of us. The soldier in the sidecar fell on the wheel. The driver got on his feet and made frantic gestures with his arms before falling on the road

From the right, a truck was coming that we had not seen. The man at the extreme right of our line saw it before I did, and he started to run. Some kind of a domino effect took place. One after the other, the eleven started running. Last on the line, I started last.

The truck stopped right in front of the sidecar and soldiers began shooting at us. The other guys were smarter than I was. They ran to their left, protected by the trees from accurate firing. I ran straight ahead in the thinner part of the grove to find myself immediately running into a potato field. Plants of potatoes, six inches high, do not provide a convenient shelter. I was zigzagging full speed among the potatoes, a symphony of whistling sounds of bullets in my ears. I was sure that I was going to fall dead, my nose in the potatoes. I did not. At the end of the field, my carbine and I crashed into a depression in the ground.

I had not even thought of dropping the carbine. I was safe. I never understood why I had not been killed in that potato field. When I started running, I was no more than four or five hundred feet away from the truck. The Germans had not entered the grove. They had remained in their truck. I supposed that seeing me falling on the ground, they believed that they had got me.

A few minutes later, Marc and the men were with me in the depression. I saw that they, too, had not dropped their weapons. I had told them that we should not expect miracles. We were watching a miracle: none of us exhibited a single drop of blood. Inexplicable! Whatever the explanation was, the German officers had no reason to be proud of the firing accuracy of their men.

Our military exploits had come to an end for the day. It was a disastrous day. I still had to evaluate the casualties, if there were any, and the practical damage. One thing, however, was for sure. The Germans didn't have enough men to surround the whole woods. One or two thousand men would have been needed to do the job. Judging by the number of trucks that we had been able to spot, there were between two and three hundred men, no more. It confirmed my previous thought. They came with the exact knowledge of our number and location. It was a concise operation aimed at catching us by surprise. Someone had betrayed us.

I was lost in speculation when Marc declared that we should move to the regrouping point. We had to walk our way back to our woods, making the same long detour. I was hungry and thirsty, and I guessed that the others were as hungry and thirsty as I was. The problem was that we had nothing to drink and nothing to eat, and there were no farms on our way from where we were to where we were going.

From afar, we ascertained that the trucks were still in the middle of the road. It was more than probable that the Germans were occupying the guardhouse, the "castle," and the dependencies. We went all the way down the hill and found our men waiting for us. Marc and I counted our force. All together, we were sixty-one men. Some forty of them had disappeared. Ten had rejoined by accident after spending the day in the woods. Among them was our "chef de cuisine." Those men knew no more than we already knew: someone screamed that the Germans were coming. Everyone ran into the woods for survival.

I was worried. I hoped that the forty men who had disappeared had gone back home or had just left us after a frightening experience. There was also the possibility that the Germans had taken some prisoners. If that were the case, there would be no way to discover the truth. The prisoners would vanish from the surface of the earth in the hands of the Gestapo without leaving a trace. Most of our one hundred were not local. The locals, we knew. As for the others, without identification, it was possible that their families would never hear of them again.

One of our immediate preoccupations was food. We had to support the morale of our chef who, at the word food, exploded in imprecations against the Germans who had unduly eaten the food that he had prepared for us. Drinking was not a problem. There was a small pond close by. We would do as the frogs do. We would drink from the pond. Marc, who never lost an occasion to make a joke, even in the worst circumstances, said that the real reason why the French were nicknamed "frogs" by the British was not because they eat frogs, but because they behave like frogs. Frogs or no frogs, we drank from the pond.

The night was now falling. We were tired, and if we had nothing to eat, at least we had a roof above our heads. The floor of the sheep stable was of uncertain composition, but it was so old, so many years had passed since sheep had occupied the stable, that it resembled granite. We could have slept on it, and it was big enough for all of us. Instead, I decreed that we had to move. The experience of the preceding morning was enough for me. The road was too close. Out of the woods, that stony sheep stable would be the first place the Germans would check if they decided at dawn to drive down the hill. After explaining my reasons, the grumbling ceased. We were again on the move.

Where to? The only place that came to our minds, Marc's and mine, was the small wood that we had already considered. From where we were, it was an eight-kilometer walk. It seemed a long, long march. We halted several times, lengthily. Around midnight, we reached the wood. We were now on that plateau that went slowly down to the river on its other side. Were Germans in the farms around? There was no answer to that question. I had enough men with enough guns to overcome a few Germans occupying a farm, but what would be the ulterior consequences of our action?

I did not dare to take such a risk, especially with a locked carbine in my hand and a band of nice, undisciplined, and untrained young men to accomplish a commando's deed, knowledge of which I had only through movies. I also considered that we could endanger the lives of farmers. The only remaining solution was to stay in the wood and wait for the light of dawn. Luck was a temperate night in June.

At dawn, Marc and I left the group. The command to the group was to stay put. We wanted to go and try to figure out the situation. We did not have to go very far to figure it out. A German truck passed on a small road that we had not seen from our position, meaning that the Germans were still there. We had nowhere to go. It was of no use to think of moving our large group, or to cut the group into smaller groups to go after food in daylight.

We had to stay together and wait where we were. Capture by the Germans would mean death. Everyone in the group understood it when we gave them the good news. The food situation was less than brilliant. The Germans had enjoyed the breakfast served for us at the dependencies, and we had had nothing to eat for the last thirty-six hours.

The previous day had been long and the night miserable. All we had in front of us was another long and miserable day without food, and that day was as miserable as the night. Our luck was the nice sunny warmth, but long were the hours before night would come again. We could not go on forever, walking to nowhere without food. I knew from Marc that there was a hamlet ten kilometers away. The hamlet had the particularity of possessing a baker who served all the farms around. I made the decision to make the bakery our next objective. What will happen will happen. At night, we could use the road. Despite our poor physical condition, we could reach the hamlet in less than two hours. Departure was fixed at ten, when the night would be dark enough, and the Germans would not be roaming the roads.

At ten, we started walking. We had to cross several fields before reaching the road. One of our men had saved "his" automatic rifle that was the heaviest gun completing our armament of carbines, Stens, and handguns. After a while, I proposed to the young man carrying the automatic rifle to make an exchange with my carbine for two or three kilometers to give him a break. I put the gun on my shoulder. The kilometers seemed to measure ten thousand instead of one thousand meters, and the gun weighed like a ton of bricks. I walked in a cotton cloud, pushing one foot in front of the other. I lost consciousness of my movements. Was it one minute or a fraction of second? I don't remember, but I woke up from sleeping while walking. I thought that I should not do it again, if I were unwilling to break my nose on the pavement.

We finally reached the bakery. It was almost midnight, and we were sixty men in the middle of the road. We resembled a caroling Christmas choir ranged in half a circle in front of the bakery, waiting for the baker to open his windows and raise his arms toward the sky in a state of anguish. I thought that we were ready to carol for a piece of bread. I knocked several times. A window opened on the second floor. Instead of raising his arms toward the sky, the baker looked down at the street. His wife appeared behind him. He understood immediately. "Wait for me!" he said. Several minutes later, he opened the door of his shop. I came in with Marc and Eugene

"You are the guys the Germans were after," he said. "I don't know if you had casualties, but those pigs killed two farmers. They beat one to death with a cow chain. What about you?"

At the point where we were, risk no longer existed. I gave the baker a brief résumé of what had happened. I added that we had not eaten for more than two days. While we were talking with the baker, his wife had come down from the second floor.

"Oh, my poor boys!" she said. "My husband will cook a batch of bread for you. Will you, Sylvain?"

"For sure!" Sylvain answered.

Both had nice open faces, both in their thirties. Hair that was missing on the top of his head was on hers. Or, perhaps it was because she had got up in such a hurry that she did not have the time to take care of her curly hazel hair flowing over her shoulders.

"Do you know what we are going to do?" Sylvain was addressing his wife more than us. "We will put those men in Joseph's barn. The attic is full of hay. They can sleep. In four hours, the bread will be done. We have plenty of eggs and some potatoes. My wife will go with you to show you the barn. You can count on us. We are with you. You can stay there tomorrow. I'll send someone to find out what happened at the 'castle.' Here you are secure and we will feed you."

The barn was an enormous wooden structure with a second floor accessible by a solid wooden ladder. There was an opening in the middle of the floor to drop hay through but it was closed. When the last one of us was on the hay, the baker's wife asked us to pull up the ladder. "I will call you when the bread is ready. Nobody will disturb you there."

We fell dead on the hay. I do not remember falling asleep. After an indefinite period of time, we were called from outside. The baker and his wife were at the foot of the barn. It was still night. We lowered the ladder. Minutes later, we were rich with ten large round breads, one egg and one potato per person, and jugs of wine mixed with water. We ate in the dark but we saw with our hands what we could not see with our eyes. That meal was the best I ever had, before or after that night.

The "chef" sided with me to declare that it was the best meal he had ever eaten. We devoured the fresh bread made of white flour that was so good that it melted in your mouth after taking possession of all your olfactory capabilities; eggs that had never had such a flavor of eggs; potatoes that had a delicately mixed smell of earth and stone. The wine was more difficult to define because it was mixed with much water, but it went down our throats as if it were divine grape nectar. Hay had never been softer and more aromatic, and we fell back, dead, on it.

It was full daylight when I woke up. The ladder was down, and Marc and Eugene were gone. The morale of the troops was much higher judging by the visages of all those young men. Rested and fed, they felt better and more optimistic. Soon Marc and Eugene showed their noses at our level.

"That baker is a terrific man," Eugene declared. "He sent one of his cousins to find out what the situation is with the Germans. We have to wait until he comes back to learn something. The baker is cooking more bread and some cakes. He said that his oven is big enough for the dozen chickens that he will cook after the bread. Everyone in the hamlet is helping with the food. They want to see us well fed before we go."

I went down the ladder, straight to the bakery, Eugene and Marc on my heels. The baker told me that he was happy to see me, and see me well rested. His wife entered by a back door. She had turned her hair into a big and elaborate chignon (bun) that suited her very well. I was wondering if she was nicer with her hair on her back or with her chignon.

"I have a bottle of 'Vin Cuit,' she said. We are going to drink it to the defeat of the green pigs and the liberation of France."

We toasted and drank the 'Vin Cuit' that was slightly rosé, with an agreeable sugary taste, and strong in alcohol. The baker opened his oven's door once in a while to see how things were doing inside. The cousin, that he had sent to gather some information, came back one hour later on his bicycle.

The Germans were gone; the place was empty. That was all he could say. He had not gone down the alley to look inside the "castle" and the dependencies. I thanked him and told the baker that we would leave after eating the wonders that he and his wife had prepared for us. We would take the leftovers, if there were any.

Marc and I agreed on one point. The Germans would not come back soon. They would speculate that we would not come back twice to the same place. That was the reason we had to come back, twice, and reoccupy the woods, but not the "castle." You never can tell! There was a *"pavillon de chasse,"* a hunting lodge, in the lower part of the woods. That would be our next headquarters.

There was a well at the lodge, and it would be possible to cook outside. Boy! Oh, boy! We had not lost our "chef." There was hope on the food side. We also could establish a decent encampment in the woods around the house. It was summer; the nights were not cold. Only rain or thunderstorms were to be feared. In fact, if we had been sure that the Germans would never penetrate in the woods, we should have established our quarters there, directly at the beginning. But it is always easy to use "if" afterward.

"We will move camp to arrive at the lodge in the afternoon. We can do it without fear, for now," I told Marc and Eugene. "We will get organized, and tomorrow morning, Marc and I will go to the 'castle' to see what is what. I have to know as soon as possible about the mission. I hope they escaped. I hope that for them, but also because I don't see what we could do without them. Still alive, they will contact us at the guardhouse. That's where we will wait. Eugene, you will be in charge while we are away."

We did as I said. We ate all the food that the baker and his wife put in front of us. They had also prepared two big bags of food to take with us, "for tonight or tomorrow," they said. "Come back to see us!" they added. I answered that we certainly would, if it were only for the bread. "Any time," the baker said with a big smile. "I will always have flour for you."

She had undone her chignon. I concluded that she was nicer with her hair loose on her back. It gave her an attractive touch of wilderness, a little something of a lioness.

The lodge was rustic but clean and in good condition. A half-kilometer path through the woods led to the road absolutely invisible from the lodge or vice versa. There was no tempting gate and alley for German trucks or cars. It was, after inspection, a much better strategic position than were the "castle" and its dependencies. I thought that we had it too easy with "la vie de château." Besides, the location of the "castle" was too obvious. Accusing nobody, including me, the choice of the castle was bad judgment. Part of the excuse was that everything went too fast after the announcement of the "invasion" to take time to think. We had let euphoria take over.

We would try not to see it happen again. First, we were immediately going to reinstate a watchman surveying the road. "Second," I told Marc, "I would have been dead with that carbine if I had had to fire it twice. With your family tradition of hunters, you are the one who knows guns. You are in charge of having guns that can shoot more than once. We still have food for today and are not starving. Let's relax a little. I will sleep outside, but we need blankets and a few other necessities. Eugene! You are in charge of the camp's discipline. It includes latrines. Do it any way you want but no odoriferous breezes around. The woods are vast enough.

You arrange that!" As I could have expected, Eugene made me understand that he felt very honored by my show of confidence.

The next morning was less relaxed. Marc and I walked through the woods up to the "castle." We arrived at the dependencies. The table was still set but empty. We definitively concluded that the Germans had eaten our breakfast. Perhaps was it an agreeable diversion from their barracks' menus? As there had been no combat, nothing had been destroyed. The car was gone.

"One lost, one found," Marc said. "I know where there is another one that runs. Any time you want."

"Perfect!" I told Marc. "But for now on, it is too dangerous. Everything on foot, even for the food, and the food at night. We'll see later about a car."

Apparently, the Germans came to kill or capture, not to destroy, but the prey had fled, I hoped. That was still one of my big worries. What had happened to the forty men who disappeared? Had the Germans captured some of them? I hardly dared to think about that possibility. The fact that they had not destroyed, or burnt the buildings, was the apparent proof that they were after nothing else than the "terrorists." It reinforced my theory of betrayal. They knew exactly what they were doing. It was not a reprisal operation, but a police operation.

We walked slowly to the "castle." The doors were open. As soon as I was inside, a strange sentiment of unreality engulfed me. I did not know if Marc had the same feeling. I was looking at what constituted their universe, imagining those two old people moving around their familiar objects. My feelings became confused. It was as if another me entered into the room where we had told them that we were going to use their property, welcomed or not. But now, at that minute, they were not in their home anymore. Only their mental images were moving, like ghosts, in my own mind. Where were they, In some jail of the Gestapo? Tortured, maybe, to make them talk about the terrorists that they sheltered and helped?

"The Germans took them," I told Marc. "We should have obliged them, even by force, to leave, instead of accepting their noble attitude. The victims, so far, are only people who were not involved directly with us, the two farmers mentioned by the baker, and those two people here."

We were stepping for the second time in a house in which we had not been invited. I shouted the classic, "Anybody home?" knowing that there was nobody home, and that the house would not answer my question. Life had left that house. It was a dead house. I did not want to go through the rooms and go upstairs. I did not look at the books lining the shelves of a library in the room where they received us for fear of discovering their intellectual preferences. I did not want to learn more about the old lady and her husband. I thought again that we had in some way abused them with our questions, and had occupied their property by force. They were certainly paying the price for us now.

"Let's get out of here!" I told Marc. "This house gives me the creeps."

"Me, too!" Marc said.

We left the house, carefully closing the doors, and walked in the direction of the guardhouse. The gate was wide open, and so was the guardhouse. Nobody was home, but nothing was broken. The attic was the same. There were no traces of bullets or bloodstains. We closed the doors. "When they heard the trumpet, they had enough time to escape," Marc said. "I am sure that they are alive. You are right. We must wait for them here. They will come back here exactly as we did, and for the same reason. They have to find us."

"What is stupid is that Mary wanted to give me her new

location," I added. "She did not at the moment, and I did not ask her. Everything went too fast. I agree with you. They will get in touch with us here and nowhere else."

I waited all day. I had sent Marc back to the lodge, and remained alone, ready to run if necessary. I left when the night was already dark. I always liked walking through the woods at night. They are much more silent than during the day. Immobile, you can hear every noise made by nocturnal animals, or hear human steps, even from far away. Nothing is easier than evaporating in the surrounding darkness, behind any of the screens provided by nature, if there were danger. I walked fast in the woods and arrived at the back of the lodge.

When I returned, "Nothing!" was my only comment. "Marc, you stay here with the men tomorrow. I'll go alone. They need you here."

The next morning, I walked again to my waiting post, just in time to catch sight of a silhouette on a bicycle coming in the direction of the gate. Of course, it was Michelle!

She let her bicycle drop on the ground. She rushed in my arms where she remained immobile for a few seconds. "Thank God, you are alive!" She could not say more. She kissed me on both cheeks. "They are alive, very anxious to know about you and your men. They are in a small farm not too far away. The guard went to a parent's farm. Tell me what happened to you, and where you are, now. I am still your liaison officer, you know!"

I told Michelle the whole story and explained where we had decided to establish our new headquarters. "You will have to show me," she said. "Right now, you must walk to the village. There is a bicycle for you at P'tit Louis', Annette's bicycle. I will wait for you there."

I walked to P'tit Louis' farm. I had to tell Annette and him what had happened. I also wanted to see my grandmother, but there was no time for that. "I already told her that you were alive," Michelle said. "Let's go."

I found Mary, Peter, and Thomas, the radioman, in a small farm twenty minutes away. We congratulated each other as if we were emerging from the kingdom of the dead. I slowed down the congratulations when I announced two dead and the disappearance of the "castle's" inhabitants. I also said that I had lost almost half of my men – vanished. I was not worried about that. If they had gone back home, I affirmed, as if I wanted to persuade myself, it was because they did not possess the "whatever it is" that makes underground warriors. I told them about our visit to the "castle," but I abstained from expressing my feelings concerning the two old persons. I did not want to bring the conversation onto a subject that could create an upset. We needed no waves in our situation. I kept my thoughts to myself.

"Now, for the rest of the story," I said, "the whole affair was a mess. We have to talk seriously. We will achieve nothing if we do not get better organized, and our men better trained."

We talked seriously for two hours. After two hours, Mary declared that she needed someone to help reorganize the mess in her whole sector of operation, especially if it were to be extended. She told me straight, her light blue eyes fixed on mine, that she had nobody other than me for that job.

I would be in charge of communications among the diverse groups of the resistance, if there were or when there would be several groups, gathering information about their needs, gathering information about the Germans, in other words in charge of the practical and material aspect of the resistance in her sector. I objected fiercely, stating that, as a future artist, it was against my fundamental nature to organize whatever it was that needed organization.

"I am here as an organizer, some kind of an administrator," Mary answered me. "Peter has his job to do that nobody can do for him. I will not explain to you what it is. Our radioman is the most precious member of the mission. Without him, we can do absolutely nothing. I coordinate the whole operation of the mission, and I cannot be permanently on the road, going from one group to another and taking the risk to disappear in so doing. Without me, and the mission, you would soon be reduced to nothing. This is why I need a man who will accept replacing me on the road when necessary."

"You don't even know me," I finally advanced.

"It's part of my job to pick the right man for the right job, and I am sure that you are right for it, by your education, and…." She hesitated, "because you are adventurous or crazy enough to do it, precisely because you are an artist. OK!" Mary concluded. "You are in charge. Anything you do, I will support. I made another decision concerning you. It will be good, if you accept the job."

As she paused, I asked, "May I know?"

"You certainly may, because I need your agreement. I am going to ask London to incorporate you as member of our mission, meaning that you will become an English officer under my command. There is one condition. The mission is here to help the resistance, not to fight with it. Sorry to say this, but you are already much more difficult to replace than a soldier of the underground. If you accept, you give up the command of your group, and choose who, in your judgment, is the best man to replace you. I suppose that it will be Marc. Tell him that we will recognize him officially as commanding the group, but that you cannot stay on with the group. You will be on your own for your practical daily life. Do you agree?"

"Do I have an alternative?"

"No, not if you want to be really useful."

"In that case...."

"Come back tomorrow. We have many things to discuss together. I have to give you a crash course on matters and technicalities concerning our job."

I also said goodbye to Michelle. She was going back to her farm. I had to pedal in the other direction.

"We keep in touch, Michelle," I said. "I will need you."

"Any time!" she answered.

Back at the lodge, I gathered all the men around me. "Men!" I began as a general addressing his troops in a movie, "I have an announcement to make. From now on, Marc is officially your commanding officer and Eugene his adjutant. From now on, you are considered as regular soldiers in the French army. If you disagree, it's time to quit."

None did.

Of course!

At first I rode a bicycle everywhere, but the distances were too great, so
I began to use the car that Marc had found, and began to visit other groups of resistance in the area.

I took the car on a path that was broad enough to accommodate a truck. It was no more remarkable at first sight than any other path opening into the forest along the road. Yet, several curves concealed the farm. At one of them, three armed men emerged from nowhere and faced the car. A broad smile came over the face of one of them.

"Ah, René!" the man said recognizing me, "They are waiting for you."

Nobody could have guessed that such a farm existed behind the trees. A vast expanse of cultivated fields extended beyond the house. The forest marked the boundary of the fields. Men were all around the buildings, many with weapons. On the right, several trucks were camouflaged under the trees; three of them were tankers with German insignias on their doors. A man directed me to drive my car into the barn on the left of the house. Inside the house four men were waiting for me. It was still early but a bottle of wine was on the table.

I must say that our relations had not happened by accident. Contacts had been established by Arabian telephone. I had agreed with Mary to visit two different men located in two opposite directions. Well! We still were in that zone of imprecision where anything, good or bad, could happen. In both cases, it turned out well. It could as easily have turned out badly. I was not ready for new experiences of the Marika type, but I had to do my job.

First, I went west to see a man named Prince. Sending back a message by Arabian telephone, I managed to fix the time and location of a meeting with him. Prince was a strong man that I estimated to be in his late thirties or early forties. He was tall and well proportioned, with a face full of energy, slightly curled brown hair, and brown eyes that looked straight at you. You could guess that he would be formidable when angry. He had the strength to support his anger. His voice accorded with his physique, soft but with controlled bursts of toughness. He did not approach the object of our meeting obliquely.

"That wine is all the coffee we have," Prince said.

"It's perfect with me," I said. "In any case, I don't like coffee."

"So, you are the British mission?"

"I am."

"You look young for the job."

"Value does not depend on the number of years!"

"Touché! You are a classicist. Let's talk business!"

"What do you need?" I asked.

After our first meeting, our relations were always friendly. The vast expanse of fields behind the farm had been approved by London as a drop site. Where supplies were concerned, I had the feeling that I was acting as a salesman taking the orders for his company, that much of this and that much of that. I had the same feeling when I was taking orders from the "commandant" who also had an approved drop site.

I had another friend at the farm, Doctor Alibert, prototype of the perfect Provençal, tall, dark hair, dark eyes, speaking with the Provencal accent. I never knew why and how he ended up in Prince's group instead of cultivating his vineyards in Provence. By principle, I never asked questions, respecting the rule that the less you know, the better it is for the collective security, but I must acknowledge that, many times, I would have liked to have asked some questions.

"OK," I said. "Here is the situation. We know that a lot of Germans are going to pass through this area, especially on this road, which is one of the few available for them to retreat from the Atlantic coast and the southwest of France. The plan is that in the near future, we will ask the 'commandant' to move and join his forces with yours. He is too far off the main roads. I am sure that you will get along perfectly well. He is a very amiable, but also a very determined man. He is also known under the resistance name of "la Blouse" for the reason that he was manufacturing womes's blouses before the war.

"You are the one who got us in touch," Prince answered. "I'll be happy to have him here. Don't forget that I have all his tankers."

I never discovered how the "commandant" had put together a team of five men who were specialists in stealing gas tankers from the Germans. Two of them spoke fluent German. Their best technique was getting the drivers drunk. The German depot was important. It supplied an airfield with aviation gas. So far, the team had stolen, one way or another, five tankers that they had succeeded in delivering to the "commandant." The "commandant" did not have the facility to make them disappear. It is where I served as a go-between. With their stealers taking risks at night, the trucks ended up on Prince's farm, with the exception of one that the "commandant" kept to supply his own group with gas.

"We will be too few to stop them if they become as numerous as you suggest," Prince said. "Talking about that, when is the next drop?"

"Soon, and you will be surprised how soon. I will come back to tell you. Marc's group will remain in its position. He can attack some of those that you will not stop and some of his own. OK! Give me your list."

Prince gave me a sheet of paper. "All that? How many are you now?" I asked.

"Last count was six hundred and ten. We need all that's on the list if we want to do the job right. And don't forget that we will have more men with the 'commandant.' We will need supplies, especially ammunition."

"Yes, but he'll bring everything he has, and he already has a lot of guns, ammunition, explosives, grenades, trucks, and cars."

"How will he do it? It's a course of thirty-five kilometers, and he has more than two hundred men, you said, plus some prisoners, and his material. He cannot move such a caravan in the middle of the day. He also could eventually be attacked by allied planes that will think that he is a German convoy."

"We have foreseen that problem," I said. "All his vehicles will display a large white cross on their roofs. London will be aware of the move. He will do it. How? I don't know. I am, myself, supposed to paint a white cross on my car to avoid being attacked by our planes. I will not paint a white cross on my car. I have less chance of being attacked by one of our planes than of being obliged to explain the white cross to the Germans. From two risks, I chose the lesser one. I have to go. I'll transmit your needs to Mary. You will hear from me very soon."

"Be careful! You are crazy to drive a car."

"I am too tired to do otherwise," I answered. "I was bicycling in the beginning, but things go too fast, and the distances between the groups are really too great. The 'commandant' joining you here will simplify my job. Don't forget also that this is the same car that the Gestapo uses. And, besides, I have my pass."

"Hope you can confuse them! Need some gas?"

"I was counting on it. If you want your materiel, you'd better give me some gas."

Prince called a man outside. A few minutes later, the gas tank of the Citroën was full. "With the right octane," said Prince. You know that it's aviation gasoline. Without adding some oil, your engine would be destroyed after a while. I now have two specialists, two German mechanics. I believe that I am going to keep them when we will have to surrender our prisoners to the Allies. They are too good, and they seem to enjoy the situation. I believe that they are in no hurry to go back to Germany. We do not even guard our prisoners. They are fenced but they know that they can go nowhere. They are not desirous to try it. We feed them well. They eat the same as we do."

"How many do you have now?"

"Thirty-two. Practically all of them isolated cases," Prince answered. "Wait a little before going because I have something I want to show you, something that you have not seen yet, my collection of fanatics."

I followed Prince behind one of the barns where a small square space had been enclosed with a wire fence. Inside the fenced space were seven men completely naked, permanently guarded by armed men.

"This is our collection of Germans' friends," Prince said. We picked them up during the past two days of commando operations at night. All of them have been denounced by "Radio London." They collaborated with the Germans for the arrests of resistants, or supposed resistants, of Jews, and of young men sent to Germany as volunteering workers. See this one, the tall one standing with his hands on his sex because we are here, and he is shy. He is a clockmaker responsible for the disappearance of at least ten people."

"What are you going to do with him?

"Oh, nothing! Just shoot him, the others, too! Perhaps they are cold during the night, but no more than the people whom they betrayed and are in the jails of the Gestapo. In any case, they will not have time to develop pneumonia. They know. We told them that they were going to be shot, but they don't know when. That way we give them time to meditate on what it is to be shot, when you are a member of the resistance, by a German firing squad."

I had nothing to say. I looked at those men. Curiously, none of them attracted particularly my attention or my pity. I just wondered, at that moment, what Daniel's fate had been at the hands of the Germans after his arrest. Looking at them, anger was coming to my heart. All of a sudden, I was taken by the same anger that I had experienced with Marika.

"It's OK with me," I said. "They deserve it. Those guys make me sick."

I left Prince to go where my duty called me. Coming out of the woods, I looked at the road. Nothing on the right, nothing on the left. I turned left and accelerated. I had to go back to the mission and give Mary the supplies list actually hidden between my skin and my shirt, not much of a camouflage if I were caught. While driving, I had to make up my mind on which road I should choose at the coming fork, right or left. I decided that luck would be the driver, as both roads would equally reach my destination. Thus, I would let my arms make the choice at the last second before the fork. The two roads offered the same sight: rows of trees, hedgerows, cows, curves and potholes, a farm here and a farm there. After a curve on the one I chose, six Germans trucks were stopped on the side of the road. Soldiers leaned on their backs, resting, or sleeping in the sunshine. Others, seated on the grass, smoked or talked. All together, no more than twenty Germans. Where were those guys coming from? I had no time to think. I had to make a full stop in front of a soldier standing, gun in hand, in the middle of the road.

"Keep cool," I thought. "Control your nerves. Keep cool." I opened the glove compartment, took the pass, and took a deep breath before giving it to the soldier with a smile.

At that point, I must provide you with an explanation about the pass. Obtaining a pass was, as you can imagine, rather difficult, if not absolutely impossible. I had not obtained the pass. I had persuaded its holder to lend it to me with the attached car for the duration of the hostilities. I must say that the happy possessor of the pass lent it to me with the most apparent good grace in the manner of a Renaissance man. It was difficult for that gentleman not to act as a Renaissance man for the reason that he was the owner of a vast authentic Renaissance castle. The Renaissance castle housed all the drawings and masterpieces of the Louvre Museum. They had been evacuated from Paris at the beginning of the war. In the midst of an occupation by enemy armies, they were resting in peace in wooden crates hidden in the castle. They were watched over by two curators. Having been myself vaguely put in charge of watching over the security of the castle, I became friends with the two curators. To tell the truth, I had not the slightest idea of what I could do to ensure the security of the castle had the Germans decided to trespass. My charge was purely symbolic, as if to say that the Resistance had a vigilant eye on the castle.

The window of one of the curators, a well-known specialist in pre-history, opened at a level that I could reach at night after climbing over the wall surrounding the castle. I was not using the main gate that was scrutinized by too many eyes. After landing in my friend's bedroom, we always went together to pick up the second curator, a well-known historian, when not curator of those drawings. The "triumvirate," as we had nicknamed ourselves, was then going down, without making any noise, into one of the cellars of the castle where a large collection of wines and champagnes was offered to our surreptitious tasting. We were choosing two bottles, usually but not always champagne, before going back upstairs, without making any noise, to the room of one of the curators. We always dedicated a first toast without remorse to the involuntary generosity of our host. Fortune of war!

It was through my friends the curators that I learned of the existence of the pass and the car. As proprietor of a "national treasure," their owner had been entitled to the pass or, at least, it was what I imagined. I gave him, in exchange, a small piece of paper on which I had written that the Resistance would, some day, reimburse him for his car, which was a "Traction Avant

(front wheel drive) Citroên." The pass was absolutely priceless. That was the reason why I did not mention it on the receipt, only the car. It was a very impressive pass, for it was signed by nobody other than the general commanding all of the German forces in France, General von Stulpnagel. I asked one of our men, who was a commercial painter in real life, to paint in white letters the words "Musées Nationaux" above the windshield. With the pass in my pocket and the sign on top of the windshield, I was confident that I could go through any German control.

The soldier read the pass and gave it back to me, but I had to believe that the signature of his supreme commander was not enough to guarantee my free passage. The soldier walked around the car and went to the trunk. He opened the trunk that was empty but for a spare wheel. He came back on one side, and the other, and opened the back doors. There was nothing in the back. He came to the passenger door and opened it. In that car, the front seats were fixed on a rectangular metal form, about three or four inches high and ten inches wide, in the shape of a reversed U. Between the two seats was a square opening. It was possible from that opening or from the door to insert inside whatever could fit in. When the German soldier opened the door opposite me and saw the open end of the open form, he put his arm into it to verify that there was nothing hidden inside.

I saw the soldier's hand passing almost through the whole open hole, but his arm was not long enough to go any further. I could not stop watching the searching hand. Suddenly, my blood stopped running in my veins. The soldier's fingers moved less than half an inch from the nose of a revolver that was under my seat. "What the hell? Don't turn white. If you have never prayed, pray, because those are your last moments on earth, and you will have a few things to explain to your Creator." But the fingers were gone. The soldier shut the door and, with a short gesture of his hand, showed me that I could go on. I answered with a smile and waved back to him. I could have sworn that the German answered my smile.

I drove very slowly for a few minutes, the time of regaining my self-control. "That was really close," I thought. "But these guys did not look like enraged fighters. Some did not even have their guns at hand. Who knows? Where were they coming from, and which road had they used? It was impossible to close up the whole area tightly. Now, I'll find the son-of-a-gun who put a revolver under my seat. Someone used that car without my knowledge. I swear to God that I will check the car every time I drive it. Had the soldier found the gun, I was dead, despite the pass. And I will never paint a white cross on the roof."

Later when I met Mary she again said to me "René! This is what you have to do, if you agree. Knowing you, you will agree."

"Because I am the only one!"

"I did not say it. You did."

Mary had received the information that three American airmen were hidden in a farm. They were part of the crew of one of the planes that had been shot down three days ago.

We had asked for the bombing of a railroad switching station to try to stop the movement of German troops and armaments. We knew that the station was defended by a lot of anti-aircraft guns because it was a vital center of communication. Everybody was blowing up the rails, sometimes the bridges, during the night, but, early the next morning, a locomotive pushing several flatbed cars loaded with workers and materials appeared. One hour later – two hours maximum – trains were again passing by. During the last two weeks, the traffic had seriously increased. Heavy guns, armored vehicles, and trucks were seen all day long moving east.

Only once had we really been able to stop the traffic, but that story was already a month old. I had been advised that an ammunition train was slowly making its way in our direction. We had immediately asked Prince to sabotage the track as much as he could to slow it down to give us enough time to get in touch with London. German soldiers were swarming like ants on top of the cars, and soldiers were posted on the locomotive, driven by a German engineer, to signal anything suspicious. Attacking the train would have been committing suicide. An ammunition train was, however, a very valuable target for the Allies. We put our hope in their responding to the opportunity. Prince had succeeded in blowing up a small bridge that had already been blown up several times, but was still not guarded by the Germans during the night. It stopped the train for two hours.

Even running very slowly, the train was nonetheless proceeding. Early in the morning, it was only a few kilometers away from the "village at the bridge." I have already told you that our village was located on top of a rise. My grandmother's house was the best point of observation from which to watch over the flat land where the river flowed and the railroad ran.

The railroad track was hidden behind the river and curtains of trees. Marc, Michelle, and I were sitting on the grass, early in the morning, in the back of my grandmother's house hoping for the impossible. Michelle was sitting between Marc and me. In some ways, she still intimidated me. I did not even dare to touch her, especially in front of Marc. We were hoping for the impossible and the impossible happened, as it sometimes does. We heard a humming. A small silvery point was moving in an infinite blue sky. A single-engine plane fell from the sky in the direction of the train. The plane made only one pass over the train and disappeared.

We immediately heard several explosions and saw smoke rise above the trees. More explosions, short cracks, and big booms, with intervals in between, following the first explosions.

"Michelle!" I said, jump on your bicycle. Go tell Mary. She will love it."

The ammunition exploded over three full days. It was our greatest success at stopping the German traffic, because we had never done any better than slowing it down for a few hours.

Later, the three of us sat exactly at the same place, on another early sunny morning. We did not sit for long. As soon as we heard approaching planes, we got on our feet. Flying at the level of the trees, three American fighters, roaring from behind us, passed near us. We waved at the pilot who passed the closest to us, and he waved back before following down the lazy slope of the hill to machine gun the round gas tanks of the airfield, some ten kilometers away beyond the railroad tracks. The view of those planes, with their white stars, was a moment of total exhilaration. Here they were, for real! The pilot who waved back at us did not know that we were working on his side, doing our best to precipitate the German defeat, but he certainly understood our gesture of friendship.

For a fraction of second, I imagined that he was going to land on the grass in front of us. We would rush to the plane to kiss him, offer him a glass of wine, and put in his hands some of the scarce flowers of my grandmother's garden to take a modest gift from France back with him to England. It was only a fleeting vision, a sweet lie. I could not imagine, at that instant, that I was very soon going to share a bottle of wine with three American airmen in the strangest of settings, and with a sudden jump in my blood pressure. A little higher rate would have meant death, but the human body is surprisingly resilient. I survived.

When she heard the fighters passing by, my grandmother came out of the house in a hurry, just in time to watch black smoke going up in the air from the burning tanks. Two or three minutes later, a small group of bombers in perfect formation carpeted the airfield with bombs. I did not look up to count the bombers as my eyes were riveted on the explosions on the ground visible from where we were.

The materialization of the Allied presence, especially seeing clearly an American pilot, even if he passed by like a meteor, was more than we could take. The four of us, grabbing each other's hands, danced a round on the meadow until my grandmother gave up. "Sorry," she said, sitting on the grass, "but I am not young enough anymore."

The day before, while I was at Marc's, one of his parents, an adjutant in the ex-French army, arrived pedaling hard on his old bicycle. He was out of breath, but very excited. I did not ask how he knew where Marc's group was. There were apparently a lot of underground communications that, with the exception of the interested people, nobody was aware of.

Anyway, the parent (Marc told me that we could have full confidence in him) was bringing important information. The airfield had been closed after the defeat in 1940, and he was the sole guardian of that empty museum. He was wondering why he had been nominated for that solitary job. He had the feeling of being a castaway forgotten on his airfield after the wreckage of the French army, but his situation had two compensatory advantages: nobody was there to give him orders, and he was close to his family.

The information was that a German car had shown up at the airfield. A German, speaking fluent French, the parent said, gave him notice that they were going to use the airfield. He had to be ready to open all the facilities when trucks began to arrive. During the conversation, the German let slip the intent of the operation: the Luftwaffe was opening a school for young pilots.

Those were magic words. There could be no more important objective to be destroyed than a nest of young pilots eager to shoot down Allied planes. I rushed to communicate the information to Mary who transmitted it to London on that same day. Mary and I guessed that the Allies were going to react immediately. It was the reason Michelle, Marc, and I were at my grandmother's house the next morning. Our guess was correct. The Allies reacted immediately.

It goes without saying that, after the bombing, the airfield was unusable as a training school for young pilots. We even wondered how it was possible that the Germans wanted to do so in our area while, geographically, the Allies were already on top of them, in Normandy. But it is also reasonable to say that military decisions do not always indicate brilliant demonstrations of logic.

The bombing, carried out with no German interception, was precise enough to be concentrated on the airfield. There occurred, to our knowledge, only one casualty among the civilian population: the owner of a cafe located at the end of the airfield. He was certainly doing a brisk business when the base was active, but he was alone in his establishment when the bombs fell that destroyed it.

When we asked for the bombing of the switching station, we had knowledge of the accumulation of German war supplies and guns that were being transferred to Germany by secondary railroad lines. During the bombing of the station, the flack shot down three planes, and Mary was advised that three airmen were hiding at a farm. They had to be rescued. She had received no news about the crewmembers of the other planes. Mary asked me to go to rescue them. She wanted me to bring them directly to her.

I let her talk and asked no questions. Relations had to be by the book. Each member of the mission carried a small capsule of cyanide in case of capture. Moral scruples about suicide were out of consideration when, sometimes, the lives of so many people depended on the silence of one person.

"You know very well that I will go," I said. "Now, show me where I have to go. I do not have to suppose that it is an operation across fields. It can't be by car, certainly it's much too dangerous in unknown territory, especially in that direction. Only on foot. How far away are they?"

"René, don't be silly! Be careful! It may well be a trap. My source is sure but it could have been compromised. There is no way that I can verify the information."

"I know. I'll be careful."

The farm was south of the bombed railroad station. South was an advantage because it spared me what could have been the most perilous part of the rescue: crossing the railroad or the town itself to go north of it into heavily German controlled territory. For the rest, it was a 40 kilometer walk. Mary gave me the directions to reach the farm where the Americans were hiding. She had managed to have what she called a "relay" ready to provide me, and then us, on both ways with food and bed. The relay was about half the distance to the farm. The physical condition of the Americans was unknown, except, supposedly, for the fact that none was wounded. Even so, 40 kilometers in insecure territory was a long stretch.

I discovered that the relay was a nice fortified house surrounded by a tall stony wall with a handcrafted iron gate. According to Mary's schedule, I had left the mission to arrive at the relay in late afternoon. A charming old man welcomed me and invited me to have dinner with him. He was dressed like and had the manners of a "country gentleman." Chicken, potatoes, and cheese, accompanied by a bottle of Rosé d'Anjou: the dinner was perfect.

"I did not cook the dinner," my host said as if apologizing." My old Alice is responsible. She takes care of the house. She lives upstairs."

The whole house was furnished in elegant rustic style. A huge room was divided half-salon with comfortable leather armchairs, and half-library with a whole wall made of shelves full of books. A small plaster reproduction of a bust of Socrates gave occasion for the conversation to touch on Greek literature. My host seemed very conversant with the ancient Greek writers and playwrights.

"And Aristophanes was right in his comedies when he contrasted the pleasures of life, love, food, and good wine with the miseries and distresses of war," he declared. "But I am afraid that the Germans will not be more convinced by that argument than the Athenians had been."

My six years of Greek in school were not so far away. I was able, to my own satisfaction, but far from the extent of the old gentleman, to hold my part in the conversation to the extreme pleasure of my host. I swore to myself that I would "put my nose" a little more into Greek literature after the war.

"I do not have many occasions to talk about the Greeks," my host said. "I live here only since the war, otherwise I was a Parisian and a married businessman. My wife died at the beginning of the war. This house was our summer residence. Alice has been in our service for more than twenty-five years. When I decided to leave Paris to come here, her luggage was in the car before mine." He remained silent for a while. I did not want to interrupt the silence. A smile came back on the old gentleman's face. "What about a game of chess? You play chess, I hope?"

"I do," I answered, "but I would classify myself in the beginners' section."

"Do not feel uneasy because I am not very good myself. But it is too early to go to bed, and I still have an excellent Armagnac."

I lost graciously but my host was much better than I was at playing chess. Two rooms in a separate part of the house had been accommodated with four small mattresses on the floor.

"The only thing I am aware of is that you will be back tomorrow with three American airmen. You will sleep in this room. Try not to be followed, but if the Germans come – and you never can tell – you will not be in the middle of the house. You can jump outside from one of the windows and exit by the back door in the wall that I showed you."

"What about you if they come and discover that we were here?"

"That will be my business, not yours, young man," my host answered with a smile. I understood that it would be impolite to insist.

"I have to thank you anyway for everything. It was a wonderful evening," I said. I wanted to add something but the old gentleman spoke before I could add anything, "For once I can do something for my country, do not spoil it with words."

I awakened at the first light of dawn. Making as little noise as possible, I was already at the door and ready to go out when a soft voice said, "Oh no, you don't leave before you have breakfast." I turned around to face Alice, a small but strong woman with gray hair and a broad smile.

"Come to the kitchen. I have prepared your breakfast.

Monsieur will not join us. He does not come out of his room before eight." Eggs, bread, butter, jam, cheese, and milk. "I get all that from the farm. It's a small farm but it belongs to monsieur. And the farmers are such nice people! We have everything we need." She put a bottle of local "gnole," white alcohol, on the table. "From last year," she said. "Help yourself. It will give you some strength for the road. The dinner will be ready when you arrive. Be careful, they are everywhere. You don't see them, but all of a sudden you bang into them. Be careful!"

When I left, the sun was already high in the sky, a sky empty of any trace of clouds, a perfectly blue and empty sky. There was also no trace of wind, not even of a light breeze. The day was going to be warm. I walked across fields, crossing a road once in a while. At one of those crossings stood a small house with a sign atop the door reading "Café." Good to know that there was a watering hole on the way. It would still be there on the way back if the Americans were thirsty. I wondered who the customers could be in such a place. There was not even a house in sight.

It was near noon when I arrived at the farm. Mary's directions were good, and I did not get lost. I did not walk directly to the farmhouse. Hidden behind a tree, I observed the surroundings for half an hour. Nothing unusual aroused my suspicion. I got up and went straight to the open door of the farmhouse. A young woman with a baby on her arms welcomed me.

"Let me call my husband," she said. "He is in the back."

The husband came, also a young man, with the strength, face, and hands of the typical farmer of the area. "Here you are!" he exclaimed. "Happy to see you! We were not sure you were coming. Except for three men, I mean those who bought them here, nobody knows that they are here, but I cannot keep them forever. Someday, someone would find out. They are in the barn behind the house. Let's have something to drink, first. You must be thirsty. It's hot today. La Denise, my wife, will bring us something to eat. You must be hungry. The guys had everything they needed this morning. They will not be leaving on an empty stomach. I don't know where you are taking them, but I am sure that you have a long way to go."

The farmer did not question me. His wife put the baby in the father's arms. She came back from an adjacent room with bread, ham, cheese, and a bottle of wine. She took the baby back, sat with us, opened her blouse, and gave her breast to her newborn.

"A boy or a girl?" I asked.

"A boy," she proudly answered.

"The king's choice!"

She had a happy smile. Her husband and I drank to the health of mother and son.

The three Americans came out when the farmer opened the door of the barn and called them. Their eyes crinkled in the bright sun for a few seconds before they could look at me. It was the time to test my years of English in school. I felt intimidated; almost unable to utter a word, so sure was I to have a ridiculous accent. I made a real effort, and finally said, "Hello!" answered by a unanimous "Hello!"

"They really looked like three men out of an American movie," I thought looking at them. They were tall, two blond, one brunette, with smiling faces (as in the movies). Not a single word of French, of course. I thought that we could encounter a problem if we were to meet some Germans, or even some suspicious French. You never can tell. "We burnt their uniforms," declared the farmer. " We found enough pants and shirts to clothe them. We also buried all they had on them. Their pockets are empty; they have no identification."

"It would make no difference," I answered, "except that now they can be accused of being spies instead of prisoners of war. They have, however, more chance with me in the clothing you gave them than walking on roads in American uniforms. But before we leave, let me give them a lesson in French language."

It had come to my mind that an elementary precaution would be to make believe that they were French by teaching them to pronounce "*Oui*" and "*Non*" correctly. I could act as if I was giving them an explanation that they would punctuate with some *ouis* and *nons*, of agreement or disagreement. After a few minutes of exercise, they were transformed into three French country boys.

We took our leave of the farmer and his wife who kissed the four of us, and we started walking in the heat of the afternoon. My Americans were not talking much, joking once in a while when repeating oui and non. I was getting only parts of their conversation. I swore that I would practice English a little more after the war.

The heat was of the type that makes you perspire heavily. After more than two hours of walking at a brisk pace, the small " Café" came into view. I made a sign to stop and hide behind a short hedgerow. No movement was visible; no German vehicle was parked around the house. We could have a glass of wine, or whatever, with no problem. It would help us to go on.

"Allons-y!" I said in French. There was no need for translation. We crossed the road and the space between the road and the house. Followed by my three Americans, I pushed the door open. My heart almost burst out of my chest when I entered the unique room that was the "café." It was full of German soldiers seated at small round tables, drinking, and talking.

There was only one thing to do: go in. Backing out would have been catastrophic. We would not have escaped immediate suspicion, and there were some forty Germans to rush after us.

My three Americans understood immediately the situation. Their reflex was the same as mine. They remained cool and smiling. It was not our day to die. Providence helped us in the fact that the only available table was the one closest to the door. We were not obliged to cross the room under the scrutinizing eyes of the Germans, who certainly would have had a good look at us. I sat at the table and the three boys imitated me. The Germans had not really paid attention to us. I got up and, crossing the room, went straight to the bar. The man behind the bar, certainly the owner, looked at a French face that was not familiar with some curiosity in his eyes. He also looked, on purpose, at the table close to the door, but his curiosity did not go any further. He gave me a bottle of wine with a smile. I could only guess the meaning of the smile.

Wine seemed to be the national French and German drink at that café. I paid and went back to the table with the bottle of wine and four glasses. And our conversation went on, cut once in a while by short silences, as would be a real conversation, also interrupted by sonorous *"ouis"* and *"nons."* I remembered, afterwards, kicking the foot of my right-hand partner to make him say *oui* or *non*. After the necessary time for a bottle of wine among farmers talking about their cows, we got up to exit slowly. I turned my head to have a last glance at the bar. The bartender was looking at us, still smiling. I turned my head back to the door, and resumed the conversation, talking loudly while going through the door, about that cow that I had bought a few months earlier.

We did not run, but on the contrary, walked casually, and finally exhaled lengthily as soon as we were out of sight. We laughed. Goodbye, cow, as nice as you were! We needed to release the nervous pressure that had been ours during interminable minutes. We were very conscious that everything could have turned ugly.

"Not a very good idea, the drink!" I finally said in my best English.

"Good, very good," one of the three answered. "Good wine."

Anything at all in our situation might have seemed excellent; for the truth was that the wine was far from good. That man was certainly making a lot of money out of the most infamous beverage. We walked steadily until we reached the relay at the end of the afternoon. The old gentleman spoke fluent English. "Don't feel bad," he told me. "At your age, I did not speak English any better than you do. My business and my frequent traveling to England obliged me to speak fluent English. Let's have dinner." I wondered for one second if speaking English was not the link between Mary and him.

Alice kissed me as if I were a member of the family. "It has been maybe three years since he last played chess. You cannot appreciate the pleasure you gave him last night. Tonight you will have only pork. They killed one of the pigs at the farm. It's forbidden, but "they" will never know. They cannot count all the pigs all the time, specially now that they seem to have some problems of their own."

There were sausages, pork roast accompanied by sautéed potatoes and Jerusalem artichokes, and a cream perfumed with Armagnac. There were two bottles of Anjou and two bottles of Bordeaux. There was also the local gnole, and a bottle of Armagnac. After dinner, when asked, one of the Americans declared that he was a chess player. When our host asked him if he was not too tired to play, he answered that he had done nothing other than sleep and eat in the farmer's barn, so that he was ready to go for the whole night if the party necessitated it. Our host smiled and set out the game.

Before starting to play, he addressed me, in French, to tell me that he had received orders to keep us for twenty-four hours. "You will leave only day after tomorrow early in the morning. We will make it as agreeable as possible for you. Alice is delighted. It's the adventure of her life."

The old gentleman told me when we left early in the morning, "Come back to see us, if you remember the place and directions. Look at her!" he added, turning to Alice. "She is crying like a baby!" Alice was crying. She gave a big kiss to the three Americans. She kissed me last. "Come back," she said. "He was twenty years younger these past two days."

Mary was waiting for us. We arrived at noon. "Good job, René!" she said. "How did it go? Tell me everything." I told her everything, including the "Café" episode. "You are as crazy as usual," was her judgment. "For the rest, we suffered a lot," I added. "I don't want to know, even if you tell me, how you managed to have us received at what we called the relay, but it was fantastic. Out of this world at war! We were on vacation in Heaven, and treated like princes."

"I have my little secrets," Mary answered. "And I will not share them with you."

"I will know someday. I promised that I would pay them a visit as soon as I am able. I am sure that I will learn something. Can you tell me why we had to stay over there one more day, or is it a secret?"

"You were more secure over there, as you say, than here. We needed that time to make the necessary arrangements for the transfer of our three airmen. It's done. They'll be going tomorrow. In the meantime," Mary added, "I have a small job which only you can do…. I need some money."

The only question I could not ask was how she had managed to let the old gentleman know that we had to stay longer in his house while I was away only for a few hours. Peter? He was my best guess. I promised myself that I would ask Mary someday.

I protested before accepting the job; but, as usual, Mary said that she had nobody else to do it. I was the only one going from group to group, and the money was the responsibility of the mission. I had no argument to oppose Mary, not even my affirmation that if there were someone not gifted for organization, I was that one. How can you ask organization from a future artist? Mary patiently listened to me. When I finished, she simply said, "OK! From now on, you are in charge of the money. Here it is, and more is coming. I need very little of it here. You'll pay for us. The rest, use your judgment to everyone's advantage."

"I need cash for many small and medium things," I answered, "but I will ask every group to keep track of what they do with the money. No report, no more money. They are all honest men. For the big things, like automobiles, we will give receipts."

"A last thing, René. I don't want to be the keeper of that money. Hide it where you want. It's your business. Just leave a note – you know where – to let me know where the rest of it will be. I do not wish your death, but you never can tell. Here it is."

She put in my hands the box that had arrived with the last airdrop. There was a considerable amount of French money in diversely colored banknotes. I just wondered if it were real or counterfeit money. I guessed it was counterfeit. If they were counterfeit, I supposed that nobody would notice the difference. There was at least the equivalent of twenty thousand dollars. I would use the money according to the number of men in each group.

There was nothing else that I could do but take the banknotes. The first man I visited was Marc because he was the closest. I told him that I had money for some of his needs, such as being able to pay for his potatoes and erase his past debts on potatoes. That would help and make us forget the days when we had nothing to eat.

"Great!" Marc said. "I gave a small piece of paper with my signature on it to an old lady who sold me three pounds of green beans and two pounds of carrots. I am going to exchange my IOU for cash. She'll be happy."

"As I am now officially in charge of the finances," I said after Marc's interruption, "I can make all the decisions I want where money is concerned. It happens, if you remember, that I have an old account to settle with a certain pork dealer who refused to help us. He even threatened to denounce me if I insisted. I am going to insist, no later than tomorrow night. I don't want you to come, because it may be embarrassing for you after the war if you participate... I intend to make him pay."

The pork dealer in question had a very nice house in one of the neighboring villages. I took three men with me in my bandit car. We stopped in front of his door at midnight. The performance went as anticipated. First, it took a series of knocks on his door before he answered. We did not look like Gestapo agents, but he caught a glimpse of faces that he associated with bandits or terrorists. I am sure that he had recognized me. He tried to close the door on my nose, but I had a foot in the door. You know, the classic ploy.

Some people have the name of their trade spelled all over their persons. He was one of them. He resembled one of his little pigs. He was too round everywhere, and the skin of his face was too pink and too shiny. He had a solid reputation of black market and deals with the Germans.

"What do you want?" he asked me haughtily.

I took some pleasure at telling him that he knew perfectly well what I wanted. When he answered me that he did not know what I wanted, I told him with a smile, "Your money."

He gave me the whole performance. He would have done well on stage. "Are you jesting?" he asked in a burst of forced laughter. When he stopped laughing, it was to declare, "I have no money to give you. I never carry cash money."

"That is the answer of rich people," I answered him. "They never carry cash. But if you don't, your banker does it for you." I stopped smiling. "Dress up! We are going to ask your banker how much cash you carry on you."

He took it very poorly and began insulting me. I told my men to catch him under his arms and bring him upstairs. If he was not ready in three minutes, they had the order to shoot him. I knew that he was not married, so we did not have to watch a wife playing for us the dramatic last scene from Act III, when everybody dies on stage, as in a Shakespearean drama. He was ready in three minutes. We squeezed him between two of my men in the back seat of the car and drove to the bank.

We had to wake up the banker who lived in an apartment above the bank. The banker appeared inside the bank to open it from inside. He was wearing a nice violet nightgown. He took an air of dignity when he recognized the man who certainly was his best customer. He asked me politely why I was coming to his bank in the middle of the night, and what he could do for me. I just wanted to have a look at his best customer's bank account, I told him.

His first reaction was purely professional. I suppose that the words came out of his mouth, automatically, without thinking about them. "Oh! I cannot do that," he said. It's against the rules. The privacy of...."

"Listen!" I said in a very polite manner, "You may suppose that if I ask you to open your bank at midnight, and come in with a gun in the back of your best customer, it is no longer a question of privacy. I suppose that this gentleman is your best customer. Am I mistaken?"

"Oh, no, sir," the banker said. "This gentleman is our best customer."

"In that case, may I see what it means to be your best customer?"

The banker took a metal folder out of a cabinet. "Here it is, sir." I liked the way the banker gave me the "sir" in a very banker like fashion.

"Thank you, sir," I said very politely. I opened the book. I thought for a few seconds that, out of drama, we were now playing a comedy. My parents had an apartment close to the Opéra in Paris, and the apartment was on top of a theatre called Comédie Caumartin. Once in a while I watched a comedy there under the patronage of my father who was in the theatre business. But I rapidly found out that our pork dealer had 600,000 francs in his account. It was more than a respectable sum of money.

"I don't want to leave this gentleman without any cash in his pocket, or bankrupt him," I told the banker. "You will count out for me only 575,000 francs, if you please."

The two spoke at the same time, the pork dealer to scream that he would bring a bandit to justice as soon as it were possible, and the banker to tell me that he did not know if... such a sum of money.... But he did not insist. My men calmed down the pork dealer, and the banker had the money in his safe. He counted the bills carefully before asking me if I intended to sign a receipt. I showed him my best smile, asked him to close his bank, and to go back to bed. While closing the door, he looked straight in my eyes. A smile came to his lips.

We were in the middle of the street. The pork dealer seemed to have given away his life. He was speechless. I would have sworn that his skin had lost its delicate pink shine.

"The resistance thanks you for your generous contribution," I said, "but don't do anything stupid, otherwise we will come back, and will not be so polite. Now, as you feel good and lighter, you can walk home. You deserve a walk."

It was the only exaction of that sort that I carried out during the whole period of my tenure as financial provider of the resistance. After the liberation, my pork dealer sued me for reparations, but lost his case when he was asked too many questions about the provenance of his money. The revenge was mine.

Once in a while, I spent the night at my grandmother's house. This time, the door was open, and Michelle was calling. I put on my pants and shirt in a hurry. I thought that I had slept too late. I rushed barefoot to Michelle. "What's up?" I asked.

"Ask your grandmother for a comb," she answered. "You look like hell."

I realized that if she had the time to make fun of me, we were not in an emergency situation.

"I need you," she said. "I went to the mission last evening to find you. Mary told me that you were at your grandmother's. She asked me why I wanted to see you, but I didn't tell her."

"I know. You come to see me only when you need me."

"Meaning that you do not see me very often. Thank God, I don't need you very much!"

I was trying to decide if she was only joking, or being slightly aggressive. With Michelle it was impossible to discern if it were in her nature to be aggressive, or if she had developed an aggressive attitude to discourage the boys buzzing around her.

"OK," I finally said. "What's the matter? Let me put on my shoes, first."

My grandmother, all dressed up as if she were going to an official reception, was busy around the little stove standing on four curved legs.

"I warmed some milk," she said. "Why don't you have some, both of you? I even have some sugar in a secret cache. I keep what remains of it for special occasions. This is one of them."

"What is the special occasion?" I asked.

"I don't know. You and Michelle being here, for example."

My grandmother was a beautiful woman with a mixture of kindness and authority in her face and manners. She had that kind of soft but persuasive voice that made it difficult to say no to her. Her table was almost as small as the stove. "You get used to small," she had commented once. She took from a buffet two nice china cups with their sugar bowl and two nicely ornamented vermeil teaspoons.

"I make no ceremony," she said. "You will have to excuse me," she added, "if I serve the milk directly from the pan. Now you can talk. I suppose, Michelle, that you did not come here for a morning milk."

Michelle explained the reason for her visit. The local "gendarmes" had contacted her. They wanted to join the resistance. Michelle was a little skeptical about their decision. They had always been at the service of the Vichy government. It is true that they were in a difficult situation. All of them had a family and were living in the gendarmerie quarters, a big building with several apartments. It was also true that they had never manifested great zeal during the occupation. They had certainly not been of great help to the Germans. They were clean in that respect. Everybody knew it. They had army status and, for the French army, the traditional enemy was the German army.

"Anyway," Michelle said, "they want to join, but want to meet with an official representative of the resistance. I told them that I would bring someone from a British mission. They were not aware of the existence of the mission. They were very surprised. They want to discuss how to do it because they will leave their families behind them. They don't want to expose them to reprisals. They have a plan that they will explain to you."

"How did you get in touch with them?"

"You are too curious. That's my secret. I don't know if you will ever trust me. Do you?"

There was again a slight shade of aggressiveness in her voice.

"OK, OK!" I said. I should not have asked. So?"

"We will meet with them at eleven at the bridge, on the other side of the bridge, the village side. We will have to cross the bridge, or the river if we don't want to use the bridge. They fixed the time and the location, if you agree to come. They said that it is a stop on one of their regular surveillance routes. It would arouse no suspicion if we talk with them at that place."

"It's ten o'clock already. We should go. We need one hour to get over there."

"Be careful!" said my grandmother when we passed the door. "Come back any time, Michelle."

Right after passing the church, we took the path down to the river. I loved that river. It represented for me two of the most wonderful summer vacations that I spent with my

118

mother and brothers along its banks just before the war. We rented a flat bark and a canoe. There were places in the river where it was possible to cross on foot. At those places where the river had no depth, the water ran fast. There were also holes several meters deep that the fish liked, and where the river seemed almost stagnant. I enjoyed fishing early in the morning when not one leaf moved in the trees, and the fish gulped at the surface. Once in a while, we were going for crayfish. Under every turned stone, we gathered several of them. The basket was full in half an hour. We had also learned how to catch, with one hand, a fish resting in a hole along the banks of the river.

I remembered one of two Parisian sisters that I had taken in the canoe. She had said that she would enjoy canoeing with me. I had known her for only two days, when we had arrived in the small town. Unfortunately, the girls were leaving the next day with their mother to go back to Paris. When we came alongside the bank to disembark, she stood up in the canoe. A strap of her bathing suit had slipped from her shoulder revealing a charming round breast. My timidity paralyzed me. I had never dealt with such a situation. I did not know what to do or say. After a little while, she put the strap back on her shoulder. She smiled. I walked her home. When we said goodbye, she said, "Next year, maybe!"

All those images were passing through my mind while we were walking. We had almost reached the river when Michelle asked me if I had lost my voice. "Is it my company that inspires you? Talking or not, we will take the next ford and will follow the other bank."

There was no road close to the river on the other side. We could travel in security as far as the bridge. Nobody was in sight. Michelle crossed in front of me. She negotiated the stones paving the bed of the river with more grace than I. She had lifted her skirt up to her waist. "You will not lose your sight seeing my panties," she said with much simplicity. I had not lost my sight but decided that she had a nice ass. From her nice legs to her flowing hair, she presented, at that moment, the image of a perfectly lovable woman. I wondered who her ancestors could have been who gave her blond hair and green eyes. Her skin was not pale. She had a healthy golden tan, maybe due to her life exposed to the country's sun. Looking at her, I thought that it was also the natural color of her skin.

It was a day for swimming in one of the deep water holes. She would not show me a naked breast. She was not flirtatious. I knew that she would be, "like Venus, wholly attached to her prey," a romantic one-man woman. Dealing with the river running between my legs, my feet on uncertain stones, the idea of such a love resembled dreaming of a small paradisiacal island in the middle of an ocean of disasters. "Venus wholly attached to her prey" was only a literary souvenir in the memory of a boy whose studies had been interrupted by the war.

Indifferent to the turmoil of the world, the river was flowing in a different world, a world of peace and beauty, on a sunny summer day. The contrast with reality was heart breaking. I was not there to enjoy the sound of running water or wax poetic about the girl walking in front of me, but to cross a river with her for a meeting with two gendarmes who wanted to be deserters.

Venus came out of the river dressed and dry. I came out with the legs of my pants completely wet. Looking at Michelle, I thought that her green eyes were beautiful. I forgot the gendarmes and the war.

"Take your pants off," Michelle said prosaically, "and squeeze them. You should have taken them off before crossing."

I took my pants off, squeezed the legs, and put them back. Michelle was sitting on the grass, legs folded almost to her chin, and her arms around her knees.

"Your grandmother is a very nice lady," she said. "She is a grande dame. I know that you are here because of the war. You are not a country boy, you will never be a country boy. I am a country girl. That's the difference between you and me. If I were to marry a man like you, I would never be able to cope with him. He would want to live in the city, and I don't like towns. I would never belong to his world. My world is here with the hay, the cows, and the chickens. That is why I don't want to love you. I will never love you, and I will see you as little as possible."

I was taken by surprise. I sat close to her, but, before I could say anything, she put a finger on my lips. "Don't say it," she said. "Let's go! We have a job to do." I thought that my head was sinking between my shoulders. I had the feeling of being a kid compared to her. She was so much more mature than I was. She had spoken without hesitation. I was somehow flabbergasted by her use of simple words to express intricate sentiments in a manner that seemed as limpid as water running in a clear brook. She was talking too fluently. Who was she?

She started walking. Half an hour later, the bridge was in sight. The last house of the village was almost touching it. Their bicycles leaning on the wall of the house, two gendarmes were talking. "If we fall in a trap, so be it!" I thought. We walked straight up to the two men. Michelle said, "René!" The gendarmes introduced themselves as André and Roland.

André explained that their unit of six gendarmes had made the decision to join the resistance. Now that the invasion had begun, they could be of help. They had devised a plan to clear them of complicity with the resistance, and protect their families against possible reprisals. If the resistance agreed, the resistance would attack the gendarmerie. The gendarmes would surrender, and the resistance would capture them. They needed an answer as soon as possible. Because of the Allied invasion, they feared that the German could mobilize them for jobs they would not want to do.

"I agree," I said. "Today is Saturday. If nothing occurs, such as the presence of too many Germans, I give you my guarantee that we will attack you Monday, at midnight. I need one day, tomorrow, to mount the attack. We will shoot automatic rifles over the roof. You will answer with blanks. We will also shoot on the walls, before leaving with you, to show traces of battle. Women and children will have to stay on the other side of the building until we are gone. Do you have blanks?"

"More than we need."

"Fire with blanks to pretend that you resisted. Monday at midnight, then! Length of fire: sporadic during five minutes, enough to pretend, not enough for the Germans to come and see what's going on. Let me tell you that you are welcome. We don't have enough professionals like you to teach gunnery to our men and give them some discipline in action. See you Monday, gentlemen."

On the way back, I tried to take Michelle's hand but she gently took her hand from mine, and we walked silently back to the mission. Mary was delighted to learn of my deal with the gendarmes. The "commandant" would be put officially in charge of the operation "Gendarme." The gendarmerie was on his old territory, and he certainly knew some of them, if not all of them.

"So, that was your little secret," Mary told Michelle. "René, you know what you have to do. As you initiated the operation, you are the only one able to explain it to the 'commandant.'"

"I know!" I answered. "As usual I am the only one available. The worst part of the story is that it is true. I am the only one. I'll drive."

"Be careful!" The two women said at the same time. They looked at each other and smiled.

"Bye, Michelle!" I said. "See you someday!"

"Bye, René!" Michelle answered. "May God keep an eye on you."

The attack on the gendarmerie was a "total surprise" for the gendarmes, and a total success for the resistance. After five minutes of sporadic but intensive fire, surrounded by a disproportionate number of assailants, the gendarmes surrendered, were taken prisoner, and driven to the underground where they became the most useful instructors and leaders.

"René," Mary said, "we have a special job tomorrow night. We need Marc as an extra for the lights. This is a mission job. Your presence is mandatory."

The following night we were on what I used to call "Marc's terrain," which was, in fact, our old drop place. The plane came on time. Peter, Marc, and I played our part as fixed lights with Mary as Morse woman. The letter was *P*. The plane circled its objective before coming back on straight course over us. I noticed that it was a smaller plane than usual. Only one parachute opened. A man, who fell in the middle of our group, replaced the attached container. It was a perfect jump. We helped him to get rid of the parachute that we folded before I put it on Marc's shoulders. The man was curiously dressed in some kind of a uniform that I could not describe. The whole scene was taking place in the middle of the night, and we could hardly see each other.

"Happy to be with you," the parachutist said. "I don't know you, but you may have seen me already." He waited a few seconds before adding, like an actor, and with the necessary egotist tone, "You remember the movie *Mutiny on the Bounty*? Well, at one time in the movie, a man falls in the sea from the highest yardarm. I am that man. I am a stuntman."

We were again out of this world, in the middle of the night, in Hollywood, and discussing in a mundane manner the filming of the *Mutiny*. I experienced for a brief period of time another feeling of unreality. It was the war that was unreal, not our discussion that seemed so casual, so natural, that only tea or drinks were missing.

"We must go," Mary said. "We cannot stay here. It's too dangerous. Marc, and you, René, go your own way. Tomorrow at the mission, René."

It was a nice way to tell me to get lost. Apparently, she did not want me to see or talk to the man, and know more than I already knew. When I showed up at the mission the next morning, our Hollywood artist had disappeared. I never heard of him afterward. Mary acted exactly as if nothing had taken place the previous night, and she made me understand that nothing had taken place during that night. It happened again several times that an individual came down from the sky, but none of the new arrivals had jumped in the sea from the highest yard of a sailing vessel. They did not remain in my memory.

The only one who had a real surprise, one night, was the "commandant." His plane was a little early, but he was very conscious that the service was not operated on the same scheduled basis as railroads in peacetime. It was a little early. So what? When the "commandant" and his men heard the plane approaching, they lighted their torches. The plane came straight to them, seeming heading for the ground, and too small to carry containers. Instead of parachutes, machine-gun bullets traced a double straight line on the ground and a bomb exploded in the middle of the space. All went so fast, the "commandant" told me, that, after finding out that miraculously nobody had been hurt, they looked at one another like speechless idiots.

There was a big and smoking hole in the middle of the space. The first thought of the "commandant" was that the British plane was also coming. He feared that the German plane was waiting for it somewhere in the sky, but there was no way to let the British plane know about the German plane. However, they had to receive the British plane. You don't ask these men to fly as far as your dropping space to tell them that the Germans took your nerves away.

When they heard the plane, they bravely took back their place with their torches, hoping that it was not a rerun of the German plane. Thank God! It was their plane. And guess what? As in a slapstick act, one of the containers ended up in the bottom of the hole. Of course! But all was well that ended well.

The second thought of the "commandant" concerned the sudden apparition of a German plane, at the right date, and almost at the right time. How could they know? There was only one answer: someone had given the word to the Germans. Who did it would remain a question with no answer. The "commandant" was well organized. Three of the recuperated gendarmes were in charge of his two hundred men. They knew every one of them and a town crier had not announced publicly the dropping one week in advance. Even if they could pinpoint one missing man, nothing could be done about it. It demonstrated once more that "you never can tell."

A later thought was comforting. If the Germans had sent one single plane, and not two or three that would have done a better job, it was because they did not have them at their disposal. And if they had not sent soldiers to trap and destroy the "terrorists" on the spot, it was because they no longer had the means to do so. The Germans were apparently in disarray. It made it more difficult to understand why there were still people who believed that the future was in the hands of Germany and collaborated to annihilate the Resistance.

Mary had asked me to be early in the morning at the mission. When I arrived, she introduced me to "Jean." She presented him as the nominated commanding officer of our whole sector. He was an active commandant in the French army. That was all I was told. By whom had he been nominated was something I would never know. "I was not responsible," Mary told me later. I wondered for myself how Prince, our own "commandant," Marc, and a few others, who were used to acting on their own decisions with a perfect knowledge of their sector and their men, were going to collaborate with someone coming from the blue to take away their hats. I also wondered, on the other hand, how "Jean" would survive their welcome.

Mary went straight, as usual, to the real object of our meeting. I had to drive the new commandant to Prince's farm. She had not mentioned that I was a member of the mission. For security reasons, I was only an anonymous driver. The idea of a commanding officer for all the groups appeared to me completely incoherent. I had not enough experience in military strategy to envision how an order given from Prince's farm could reach Marc on time for an emergency. There were no telephones, and no permanent liaison, except me on a very erratic schedule. On top of it, the enemy was extremely fluid, and its appearance largely unpredictable. How could the new commandant know that

Marc was under attack, for example? But that was none of my business.

My business that morning was a course of 40 kilometers with our new commandant. A week before, I had delivered to Prince a laconic oral message from Mary, advising him that he should wait for me around 10:00 a.m. that day, and by all means find out why if I did not show up

I assured the new commandant that I would be delighted to drive him. It was not the usual military etiquette to answer, when receiving an order, that you would be delighted to accomplish it. I never wanted to be a soldier. I never felt like answering Mary with a well articulated, "Yes, sir!" or, "Yes, ma'am." And I did not feel like answering the new commandant with a "Yes, sir!" I must say that the new commandant looked at me with a strange expression on his face. He certainly considered me, at the moment, as a practical joker, a bad specimen of French warrior. He was not, physically speaking, a remarkable individual. Rather, I should describe him as an unremarkable individual. Everything about him was medium: size, length of brown hair, voice, and, I supposed, intelligence. You can argue that I was biased against a man who was intruding into our lives to tell us how to conduct them. It's possible, but my first impression was not of shared affection. Anyway, we hit the road after an hour of talks between Mary and him.

At this point, I must give an explanation. The road to Prince passed through the most important agglomeration of our sector, where the address of my pass was precisely located. It was a nice small town with hotels and stores. To reach it, I could use the main road that crossed it further on, or the back roads, which was a little longer but supposedly more secure. It was, at least, what I thought when leaving the mission.

I let the new commandant know about the choice of itineraries. He answered me that, in his ignorance of the local geography, the choice was mine. While I drove, I expected questions about the groups, what they were doing, and so on, and so on, but, after a while, I deduced from his silence that he was certainly keeping his questions for more important people than me. We drove at a low speed. You never can tell! Finally, we had the town in sight. I stopped the car to have a look at it, by precaution. Nothing seemed abnormal. "Let's go, gaily!" I said cheerfully in a very unmilitary manner.

We were still some two kilometers away from the town. Three more curves, and we would be in town. Negotiating the last curve, I stopped as calmly as I could when the aperture of a gun belonging to a tank located itself right in front of my windshield. There was nothing to be done, or attempted. I would have sworn that the new commandant's face changed colors

We did not have to wait. An officer came to my window. He was not articulating a single word of French. As neither the commandant nor myself were articulating a single word of German, the conversation was brief. The officer signaled two of his men to sit on the front fenders, and an imperative finger showed me the direction of the center of town. I drove slowly to avoid losing one of our guardian angels on the pavement. It would have been inopportune. We arrived in that equipage at the crossing of our road with the main road. A tall man in uniform, the perfect model of an arrogant Nazi officer, stood in the middle of the crossing. In front of him was a file of stopped tanks and trucks, all the trucks with large Red Crosses painted on all surfaces that were perceivable from the sky and all sides.

Before arriving at the crossing, I saw a dozen men aligned against a wall. One of them was a thirteen-year old boy that I knew. Two officers were interrogating the group. I heard the word "terrorists," while they slapped one or two of them at random. Half of the men against the wall knew that I was a "terrorist." None spoke. Curiously, the Germans let them go after a while. Most of the inhabitants had fled before or when the Germans entered town.

A long wall ran on the left side of the road. We were now facing the convoy, as was the "Nazi" commanding officer, who was effectively wearing a SS uniform. He ordered me with a gesture of his hand to park the car against the wall.

This being done, none of the soldiers around paid any attention to us, the Nazi officer still standing in the middle of the road. We had reached the town half an hour too early. Had we arrived later, we would have discerned the smoke of the first fires when I stopped to look at the town to check if everything seemed normal. In fact, that glorious armored German division, or whatever it was, was busy looting. Everywhere, in total confusion, soldiers carried bottles, radio sets, and an unimaginable array of absolutely useless items that they dropped on the pavement or threw into their trucks.

There were several houses that they were pillaging on our opposite side of the road. When they finished breaking or taking, they came out of the houses and threw incendiary grenades inside. The houses began to burn. After a while, the roof of one of them literally exploded.

While watching that insanity from the car, another drama developed in my mind. I knew that if I passed the wall with the car and the curve at the end of it, we would be out of shooting sight of the soldiers who surrounded us and looted. Some of them were certainly too drunk to aim correctly. If I succeeded at passing the wall, those who would see a car coming in front of them would never imagine that it was not one of their own cars or a friendly car. I also knew of a small path on the right-hand side, past the convoy, which I could use to be far from their reach before they could react. It was a plausible plan that had one chance out of two to succeed.

The car was in excellent condition, and the engine still warm. It could start at the first pull of the starter. But... the gas gauge was practically at point zero. In theory, I still had enough gas to go on for twenty miles, well enough to refuel at one of Prince's tankers. I was not anxious when I left Mary, because I had gas waiting for me, but, seeing the gauge at zero at the foot of the wall, tempered my desire to pull the starter. What if the car refused to start? What also if I had not enough room to pass on the side of the convoy? A second consideration had more weight in my decision to do nothing but wait: the hostages against the wall. From where we were, we could not see them, and I had no idea of what happened to them. What, also, if all the inhabitants had not fled? If my escape plan with the car succeeded, what about them? I was putting lives at stake. I remained immobile

Our only satisfaction, at least mine, was to watch one of the German soldiers mishandling an incendiary grenade that blew up almost in his face. His uniform did not catch fire but the man screamed, a scream that I will never forget. He disappeared screaming in the direction of the convoy. He was disfigured. Our standing officer shrugged his shoulders. In peaceful circumstances, I would not kill a fly, but I wished that all of them mishandled their grenades. The soldier's face was not nice to look at. I hoped, despite myself, that his pals would put an end to his life.

When we parked against the wall, the new commandant said in a low voice, "We are dead! They are going to kill us." He was not aware of my pass. I said nothing. I still had confidence in my magic pass, but I wanted to observe his reaction. I was not braver than anyone else, we were in a lousy situation, to say the least, but as long as there was life, there was hope. Those were the words of a popular French saying, and I was trying to boost my morale. The new commandant seemed to have adopted the reverse attitude. When I exposed my plan of escape and asked him for his opinion, he did not answer. He was shrinking in his seat. I hated him.

By nature I am slow to get mad but, when I get mad, I get mad. After more than two hours, with the Germans still paying no attention to us, and the commandant shrinking more and more in his seat, I got mad. I believe that I got mad more because of the new commandant than because of the Germans.

In a movement of absolute irrationality, I got out of the car, and went straight up to the Nazi officer. Arrogance for arrogance, I started almost to yell at him, declaring that I was fed up sitting like an imbecile against the wall. He had to let me go for the reason that I had my duty to accomplish as curator of national treasures. All of a sudden, I shivered. Looking at me and estimating my age, how could he believe that I was in charge of national treasures? And what was I supposed to accomplish for the national treasures driving on that road, if he asked?

Apparently such thoughts did not reach his mind. I still had to go on with my role as curator of national treasures. I told him with a more moderate voice that I had a pass signed by his superior officer, the supreme commander of all the German forces in France, General von Stulpnagel. I presented him with the pass.

He took it, looked at it, and told me in fluent French, "There is only one thing that you ignore, monsieur, my superior officer, as you call him, General von Stulpnagel, has been fired by Hitler. Today, your pass is invalid, and I tear it apart."

Luckily enough, I had no time to comment. With a violent movement of his left hand accompanied by a strong word uttered with a strong voice, he ordered me to get lost. I went back to the car, opened the door, and tried to sit down. I did not have time to sit. A soldier grabbed me by the neck of my shirt to pull me out. He said in French, "Out, but not the car!" I got out, walked around the car, opened the passenger's door, grabbed disrespectfully my new commandant by the neck of his shirt, and said, "Out, but not the car! Let's go! Move!"

We walked along the wall, straight in front of us instead of taking the opposite direction. Taking the opposite direction, and turning our backs to the convoy, would have lacked dignity. It would have been leaving the stage with the tail between the legs. I preferred taking an unnecessary risk to exit with a remnant of panache in front of the Nazi officer. I could not help it. My new commandant was walking at my side. We had to walk along the convoy made of a mixture of tanks and trucks, exactly as we had seen them when arriving, but none of the soldiers paid any attention to us. They certainly thought that if we were walking in town, we had been authorized to do so.

It was not exactly a promenade. The main street burned; all the houses were aflame. I turned into it. We had less chances of meeting Germans on a burning street than continuing on the road along the convoy. One could never tell what would occur in the mind of one of the drunken soldiers. According to the reaction of their commander at the sight of his own burned and disfigured soldier, our lives had not much value.

We walked in the middle of the street between two walls of flames. It is of no use to describe burning houses: the noises, the crashes, and the smoke. The heat was tolerable. Going straight would lead us toward freedom. We just had to cross the piazza and cross the street at the end of the piazza. After that, we were out of town.

There are reflexes that you do not govern. We were on a sidewalk that made a right turn at the end of the last house on the piazza. We just had to go straight across the street. I suddenly stopped. The new commandant stopped behind me. I showed my nose at the corner of the house. I backed off instantly. A volley of machine-gun bullets scratched the stones at the level of my nose.

"The guy was fast!" I said to my new commandant. "We cannot cross the street as long as they are there. Here is a bench. Let's sit down and wait."

There was absolutely nothing that we could do, and nothing that I could say to the new commandant who was as mute as a carp. I did not even feel like talking to him. The man had no class and no guts. The houses were still burning but, being built in solid stone, the fire did not pass from one house to the next to destroy the whole town. I supposed that only the houses that had been set aflame with incendiary grenades were burning. We waited, and waited, and waited until we heard the noise of the German column moving away, which took a rather long time. The town was now empty. The castle had not been touched.

"Commandant," I said, "we must go around town and see what the situation is. Maybe we can help. Don't you think that it is part of our work to help when a catastrophe happens?"

The fire had been limited to one street, the street we had walked through, and to the few houses that had been put afire while we were in the car along the wall. The new commandant and I found two bodies in the streets, two men, but no witnesses to their death. Perhaps they were just killed at random, being at the wrong place, at the wrong moment? With the Germans, no predictions were possible. They could kill or spare a life at their leisure. I assured the new commandant that we did not have to take care of the two bodies. Parents or friends would do it

While we were exploring the town, some inhabitants were slowly reappearing. From the hills around town, they had seen the fires, and also the German column moving away.

There was another piazza in town, a smaller one that we reached at the end of a street. Alone, in the middle of it motionless, stood a young woman who called to us as we were entering the piazza. Curly hair framing a spiritual face, a funny little nose, two almond-shaped hazel eyes, she looked, in the middle of a town that had gone through the devastation of the German armored column, like an apparition from another world. I believe that my mind had a tendency to escape into the unreal in order to forget the intolerable reality of war. Much more than physical, my denial of war was intellectual. I was finding a refuge in anything, any image that could, one way or another, give some food to my antiwar imagination.

Nonetheless, the young woman was for real. She said, "You do not know me, but I know you. You pass by town with your car once in a while. There is no one else but you who does so. Am I mistaken if I say that you are an important member of the resistance?"

"So much for the secret," I thought. "I have to tell that to Mary. "Where were you when the Germans came?" I asked.

She said, "Someone shouted in the streets that the Germans were coming with tanks. In five minutes, the town was empty, or almost. The inhabitants fled to the hills. My mother and I didn't get that far. We went across the street and beyond the gardens where nobody could see us. We waited. The Germans never came over there. They did not put houses aflame in our part of town. We could hear them, but we could not see them. We heard them moving away.

When we could not hear anything anymore, we came out of hiding. And here I am."

"I don't know about you, but I need a drink. All that is too much!" I told our new commandant. "We have to wait, anyway. We have no more means of transportation. Prince's men will come to pick us up, but give them enough time. We don't know what happened with them. What is your name?" I asked the young woman.

"My name is Melody," she answered with a smile.

"Melody is not really a French name."

"No, but I like it." And she added, "I am happy to meet you despite the circumstances because I did not know how to get in touch with you. I could not stay for days in the middle of the road waiting for you. I never had an occasion to stop you. We want to help if we can. "We" is my two girlfriends and me. Follow me."

She took the lead and we followed. She knocked at the door of what seemed to be an ordinary house. I noticed a small sign on the side of the door. When the door opened, we were in a minuscule café. The whole establishment consisted of one table in the middle of a small room. A woman was there who asked us if we wanted to drink.

"Don't you think that we have more important things to do?" asked the new commandant. After his demonstration of courage in front of the Germans, I was in no mood for his remarks. "No, we have no more important things to do than what we are doing now," I replied. "It will be enough, in a while, to go on the road to wait for Prince's men. Prince knew that we were coming. He will send some of his men to find us, anywhere we may be. Beside, it would be impolite to refuse an invitation of a young lady. We would make a breach in the reputation of the gallantry of the military for the ladies. Besides, this young lady and her friends want to help us. We always need all possible help. Perhaps have you noticed that we are not a regular and well-disciplined army? Our methods of recruiting are unorthodox."

The new commandant did not react to my unfriendly answer. We were served a glass of wine. It did not occur to me for one second that the so-called Melody was not a genuine and honest French girl.

"My father is a prisoner of war in Germany," she said. "I want to introduce you to my mother. You'll come to my house. But, tell me how my two girlfriends and I can help."

I knew how they could help. "Are you ready to leave your home and see blood?"

She looked at me, intently. "Why?"

"Because I have a friend who is a doctor and lives in the woods to take care of our wounded men and the wounded Germans who are our prisoners. You know perfectly well that there are a lot of skirmishes around. There are wounded men on both sides. Sometimes, the Germans do not have time to pick up their wounded. They abandon them. In short, if you want to serve as nurses, there is work for you."

"I don't know about my girlfriends, but I will go. First, you have to talk to my mother."

"First," I said, "We have to leave this place and go back on the road. Let me pay, and we go. Let's go on the road at the entrance of town. Prince's men will not miss us."

"I will go with you," Melody said. "But I want you to meet my mother before I go with you to meet your doctor."

We walked slowly for ten or fifteen minutes before a car showed up. "We were right on time. See!" I said, addressing our new commandant, "Wine was dripping in the hourglass of our destiny to indicate a perfect timing. It's how we measure time here in combat operation." I was mean. I almost regretted torturing that poor man but, remembering the wall, I had no pity for him. In fact, I would have put him in jail for treason in front of the enemy.

The car was driven by two of Prince's men. I knew them. "Happy to find you," one of them said. "The boss was very anxious about you because you were supposed to arrive around ten. That German force surprised us. We attacked them, but we are not equipped to fight tanks and their guns on flat ground. We did not stop them for long, but we stopped them. We have several wounded. We are afraid that what we see here is reprisal."

"Before we go, we have to make a stop. Melody, show us where you live."

Melody's house was uptown, a small but nice little house. Melody's mother was the image of her house, small and nice. Her daughter was taller than she was. A family look linked the two women.

"I know!" Melody's mother said. "She wants to go and help. She is nineteen now. I cannot stop her. It would be wrong. She would resent it for the rest of her life... and mine. Well, she can go. I put her in your care. I believe I can trust you."

"You can," I said. "She will come with us, now. She will be back tomorrow. I want her to meet my friend the doctor to see if she still wants to do it, but then, after that, she will have to live over there." Addressing Melody, I said, "Melody, go pick up a blanket for tonight."

Her mother took my arm. "Her name is not Melody..."

I interrupted her. "I know," I said. "But I don't want to know her real name. From now on, she is Melody, and it's enough."

The meeting between Prince and the new commandant was rather formal, with no demonstrations of sympathy. The new chief did not subjugate Prince who certainly considered his intrusion without amiability. "Wait until I tell you about the wall," I thought. I was sure that, in any case, Prince would accept orders from none other than himself.

Melody and I went to the barn that had been transformed into a hospital by my friend doctor Alibert. The doctor and I fell into each other arms, but almost immediately he asked me, "And who is that young person? I don't have time for socialites."

"Her name is Melody, your nurse, if she can do the job. She has two girlfriends who may join. Melody can stay here for the night. If she can make it, someone will drive her back home to pick up her things and see her two friends."

"It's God Himself who sent you here," Alibert said to Melody, "and God knows how much I need someone like you if your heart is strong enough to look at blood and have blood on your hands. I had twelve wounded men here, and now five more from today. When do you start?"

"Right now, if you want."

"That's my girl!" Doctor Alibert shouted, sending his two long arms around her waist and lifting her off the ground. He kissed her on both cheeks. "Now, to work! Go outside and wash your hands carefully. Where did you find her?" he asked me while she was leaving. "Never mind! You could not bring a better gift at a more appropriate time."

I rejoined Melody who was washing her hands at a pump outside. "Are you happy? Isn't that something you wanted to do?"

"It's wonderful!" she answered. "I'll be useful. I am sure that my friends will join. But promise me that you will see me when you come here." She took my head in her hands full of soap, stood on the tip of her toes, and put her lips on mine, briefly. She turned and kept washing her hands.

Prince provided me with my reserved Citroën. I had to go to the mission and give my report to Mary about the armored convoy. All together, six hours had elapsed before I hit the road again. There was enough time between the

German column and me not to meet twice in one day. In any case, my road to Mary and the German column's road were not the same. I was not taking any risk.

I learned later what had happened during those hours. Marc had a permanent force of twenty men ready for combat at the end of the path leading to the hunting lodge. He often joined his men on duty. He was with them when he saw the German armored column coming, preceded by a car that he recognized at first sight because of the two words painted above the windshield.

"Damn it! They got him!"

A formidable rage rushed through his whole body. That's what he told me afterward. He also told me that he did not take into consideration that tanks were forming the head of a column of trucks, maybe full of soldiers. He had an easy way of retreating into the woods, but he had, first, to show those Germans that they could not take or kill his friend René with total impunity. His armament was somewhat light in front of an armada of tanks, but he had a new weapon that could stop the first one. At the last drop, he had discovered a bazooka, not two of them, but one with a half-dozen rockets. The main problem was that none of his men had seen such a thing before, or had been trained to use it.

Marc had put in charge the man that he supposed was the best for the job. From Peter's explanations, the bazooka was a powerful weapon. It was a tube able to launch a 3.5-pound rocket that could penetrate the armor of a tank. The main inconvenience was that it was heavy and had to be served by two men: one who held it on his shoulder, half the tube protruding in front of him, half at his back, aim and fire, and one who inserted the rocket into the tube. But that was not the worst part of the story. The bazooka had a very short range, not much more than 110 to 120 yards. In other words, to be effective against a tank, you had to wait to fire until the tank was almost stepping on your toes. This required the user to possess nerves of steel and the training necessary to recognize the best points where to hit the tank to disable it.

Marc's two men had the spirit, but not the sufficient nerve to let the tank approach close enough to have a real chance of destroying it. Their training had consisted of firing one rocket to verify how the thing worked. It had given them a sort of false confidence in their strategic power, which disappeared when the German tank approached closer and closer. The convoy had not seen them. The driver of the "National Museum" Citroën was largely ahead of the column and he did not stop after passing Marc. Now, Marc and his men faced the first tank. Beside the bazooka, Marc had set four automatic rifles and the rest of his men with carbines. They had orders to wait to fire until the bazooka had fired.

When you are not used to seeing a tank coming in your direction, it always seems that it is coming straight at you, even if it is not completely true, and your nerves can take it only to a certain point. In the case of Marc's men, the point was a little too far off. The rocket exploded in front of the tank. The tank was manned by well-trained soldiers who calculated the departure point of the rocket and returned fire. Before Marc's men could attempt firing useless bullets against it, a gun shell exploded near their position. They retreated at full speed. Luckily enough, the trees protected them. Three men were nevertheless wounded, one in the leg, the bazooka handler in his right arm, and his server in his left shoulder. None of the wounds were life threatening, but they needed immediate medical attention, especially the leg's wound.

The German column did not even stop to check the site of the ambush. When they were gone, Marc with a dozen of his men went back to their position. All their weapons were still there, including the bazooka.

Marc reconstituted his watching group with other men. He took the bazooka out of service for the moment, he said.

Marc learned from Michelle that I was alive, and that I would visit him soon. When I arrived at the mission, Mary was unaware of what had happened during the afternoon. I told her the whole story. She said that she was immediately communicating the position of the armored column to London. I also told her my sincere appreciation of her "new commandant Jean."

She let me talk. Her only comment was, "You go back to your grandmother, and you get some rest! I don't want you on the road any more today. I will send Michelle tomorrow morning to Marc. It is very possible that the column passed by his position."

Michelle told me later that Marc danced like a mad man for a minute or two. We fell into each other arms when I came to see him at the lodge two days later.

"Now, I must take care of my wounded men," Marc told me when our effusions ended." I made the decision to drive them to the rectory, which was the closest and best place to keep them. They are in the schoolroom. Father Durand is taking care of them. Michelle went to alert Doctor Duprieux. He came three times, but he would prefer to have them transported to the hospital where he practices twice a week. He said that he would manage their admission, would sign all the necessary papers, and would have them put in isolation as contagious patients. Your grandmother has turned into a permanent nurse, and Michelle into an occasional one. We found enough ether, bandages, and whatever else is necessary in the closets of the farms around, but I am upset. The rectory is not a safe place. Let's go over there. No car. I already took a risk with the wounded. It's no use to take another one. We walk."

We walked. One hour later we were in the rectory. The schoolroom had been transformed into an infirmary. Our three men were lying on mattresses. My grandmother was happy as usual to see me. Michelle was there. She kissed me on both cheeks, and Father Durand kissed me on both cheeks. Both knew what had happened to the new commandant Jean and me. I was still talking with them when we heard some kind of a commotion coming from the village's piazza. "Let me see," Michelle said. She came back seconds later. "Germans," she said. "A lot of them."

"Damn it!" Father Durand said, forgetting at that instant that a priest is not supposed to use such words – at least in public. "The wounded, the shack!"

"Damn it!" my grandmother said, forgetting her dignity. "Their guns!"

We understood immediately. Two of the wounded got up to walk through the courtyard, forgetting their pain. Michelle opened the door of the small shack standing at the end of the courtyard. We pulled the man unable to walk on his badly wounded leg on his mattress, grabbed the two empty mattresses of the others, and literally squeezed men and mattresses in the shack on top and among the mess already there. I made a sign to Marc to disappear. He jumped over the wall surrounding the yard. Then, we went back inside the school. An odor of ether was still floating in the classroom. My grandmother had put three guns in her bag, a large bag that seemed to be made of tapestry with floral motifs.

We were back just in time to hear someone knocking at the door. My grandmother, her bag at her arm, opened the door, and went outside to meet a German sub-lieutenant. She had recouped her dignity to examine him as if she were

142

a superior officer on inspection. He looked almost disconcerted. In his late forties, already gray haired, a real German type in a dusty uniform that was less than glorious, he spoke a good French with a solid German accent. He asked my grandmother what was the building and who she was. His tone was firm but polite.

"It was a school before the war," she answered him. "I was the schoolteacher. But the school is closed. There are no more students since the war."

"Is she your daughter?" the German officer asked, showing Michelle.

"She is my granddaughter. And this one is my grandson," she added pointing a finger at me.

Father Durand and I had chosen that moment to show up. The German looked carefully at us and asked us if there were "terrorists" around. I answered him that there were, of course, no terrorists around. At that moment, a German soldier joined us to say something to his officer. A bandage was wrapped around his right hand. My grandmother jumped on the occasion.

"Are you wounded?" she asked.

The sub-lieutenant translated. The soldier answered that yes, he was wounded. One of his fingers was hurt, bad looking, and the pain extended as far as his armpit. The officer added that he did not have what was necessary to take care of the wound.

"He cannot stay like that," my grandmother declared with authority to the officer who did not know any more what to do or say. "Let us take care of him." Addressing Michelle, she said, "Michelle, please take care of that man; disinfectant and a new bandage. Now, if you allow me, sir, I will go back to my home on the piazza."

"Certainly, Madame. Let me call one of my men to accompany you, so that you will not be importuned by any of the men on the piazza. And thank you for taking care of my man."

I thought that my grandmother was going to say, "My pleasure," but she abstained. And so, she went back home, carrying in her bag three terrorist handguns. Michelle understood my grandmother. She took the German inside the schoolroom. The man, in pain, did not pay attention to the ether smell of the room. Two minutes later, the room was again filled with a new profusion of ether vapors. No one would wonder, afterward, if there were a search, about the smell. The German officer thanked Michelle. He looked at me again, and asked me if he could find something to eat. I told him that we could manage to provide him with some food.

"Follow me," I said.

I wanted to get him away from the school and the shack. The only place where I could provide him with a meal was at Marc's grandparents. We had to go back in the direction of the piazza. Some sixty German soldiers were sitting there, resting, sleeping, in total disorder, nothing comparable to the brilliant German army parading in the conquered capitals of Europe. They did not even wear the same uniform. I was not sure that all of them had weapons.

"Bicycles?" the officer asked me. "Do you have bicycles?"

I answered him that I would be delighted to provide him with sixty bicycles to allow them to go back to Germany. Unfortunately, a group of German soldiers passing through the village a week before had already requisitioned all the available bicycles. No German soldiers had invaded the village in search for bicycles, but I knew that bicycles were articles now held in high esteem by retreating Germans.

My German was not stupid. "Are you in such a hurry to see us away?" he asked me.

I did not have to answer. We had arrived at Marc's farm. When they saw us coming in, his grandparents marked no surprise. They had seen the Germans invading the piazza, and they supposed that my reason for bringing the German officer in their home was certainly in connection with the presence of the wounded in the rectory.

"Can you provide a lunch for this gentleman?" I asked with my best smile.

Marc's grandmother got busy preparing a lunch. There was plenty enough food on the farm. Marc's grandfather was playing the game. He put a bottle of wine on the table with three glasses.

"There are no enemies in front of a glass of wine," he said.

"Will you accept lunch in my company?" I asked the officer. "Can we be less formal? My name is René. Yours is?"

"Albert."

"What about your men?" I asked.

"They are like me."

"Perhaps we could do something for them. What about boiled potatoes? I am afraid that it's all we can offer to sixty men."

"They would find that unexpected and comforting."

"I still have two bags that we could use," Marc's grandfather said.

"I need to tell my men," the officer said. "Allow me."

He went out, talked to one of his subordinates, and came back to the farm. While he was away, I asked Marc's grandfather for one of Marc's revolvers. I put it in my pocket and sat down again at the table.

"Where do you come from, Albert?" I asked. "You will not betray any military secret if you tell me where you come from."

They were coming from the Atlantic coast, but were not in combat units.

"I am an attendance officer. All my men are in auxiliary services. None of them is a young man. I became a specialist in supplies for hospitals and reeducation centers. I knew nothing about the trade. I am a mathematics teacher. I learned the job when they sent me to a casino transformed into a hospital."

I listened to the man with the greatest attention.

"After that, they sent me south. That's where we are coming from, Bordeaux. In the beginning, it was wonderful for me. I don't mean... You know, there were all those poor wounded young men arriving daily. But the beach at La Baule and the whole backcountry are so nice! The casino is equipped with a magnificent kitchen that was very useful as the hospital's kitchen. I must say that as long as I have been over there, the cooks were taking great care of it. I had to provide everything, from surgical instruments to cabbage and potatoes. Do I know that place? Every inch of it!"

"Yes," I said, "when you were going downstairs to go to the kitchen, you had to turn right because there was a wall on your left..."

"How do you know that?" officer Albert interrupted me.

I took some time to answer, enjoying the surprise visible on his face.

"Because I helped my father to build that wall. My father was the director of that casino. And you don't know what is behind that wall that we made thick enough so that no one could suspect anything. Behind that wall is the whole wine cellar of the casino, hundreds of bottles of fine wines and champagnes. We left racks full of the cheapest bottles in front of the wall to pretend that they represented the wine cellar. You don't know what you missed."

There was a silence, the time, I supposed, for officer Albert to add two and two together to make four. The world is very small. Strange things happen, such as the meeting of two people who went down the stairs leading to the kitchen of a casino. It was the appropriate time to take Marc's gun out of my pocket. I put it on the table. Officer Albert had a gun at his belt, but he did not move. He smiled.

"All right, I am a terrorist, as you say. Let's put our cards on the table. I have absolutely no intention of killing a man who did not drink my father's wine. What will you do if I just let you go, now?"

"Cards on the table? Nothing. I am fed up with that war. Have you seen my men? They are just as tired of the war as I am."

"Do you want you and your men to be made prisoners? I can do that. I am not a regular terrorist. I am a member of a British mission. I can speak in the name of the Allies. Your traveling will end here. You will be well treated. I give you my word."

While talking, I took Marc's gun off the table and ostensibly gave it back to his grandfather. We had no interest in taking sixty prisoners. The only group close enough to capture them and receive them was Marc's, but Marc was not equipped to keep them, and feeding them would be a burden. The best solution was to let them go.

"Your offer is generous and tempting, and I am sure that you would keep your word," officer Albert answered, "but I cannot accept it. My men want to try to go back to Germany. You will tell me that it's a long way to go walking to Germany, and walking in hostile territory. But as their commanding officer, I owe them that. I am still a soldier, even if I do not believe in the German victory, and hate Hitler. I have never been a Nazi, and I'll be happy when all that will be over – if I am still alive! And if I am still alive, I will teach mathematics again."

"I don't believe that you will be able to reach Germany," I said. " Right now, you are free from any immediate attack in our area, but, after that, you will be on your own."

At that instant, Marc's grandmother announced that a full cauldron of potatoes would be cooked in half an hour, and she put three plates on the table. Marc's grandfather shared the food with officer Albert and me.

"You have enough time to eat," I told officer Albert. "Please do! Don't feel bad because we cannot offer your men this menu. We will add some wine to the potatoes. Just imagine that you are my guest in our casino. What a coincidence!"

Officer Albert was visibly starving. I let him eat without talking. It was almost a pleasure to watch him eating. It would certainly be some time before he would find such a meal on his way to Germany. Finally I broke the silence, "Tell me something while we eat. You said that you hate Hitler. Why Hitler? Why war?"

"Well! Germany was on its knees at the end of the war, and the twenties were a disaster. Everybody did not like him but enough people believed that he was the only man able to get Germany out of the pit and give work and food to everyone. I was a Catholic. Even the Catholics voted for him. They were persuaded that Hitler would protect them from the atheism of Karl Marx's doctrine and save them from its danger...."

"The potatoes are cooked," Marc's grandmother announced, interrupting a conversation that was not of great interest to her. "Those potatoes are like the carrots of the message from London," I thought. "They are cooked." Officer Albert excused himself. He went outside to call two of his men who came to pick up the boiled potatoes in a big cauldron suspended outside. Marc's grandmother utilized with unintentional irony that particular cauldron. It was the only utensil big enough to cook potatoes for sixty men above a raging wood fire, but it was also the utensil she used to cook the pigs' food. Marc's grandfather added ten bottles of the wine from the cask kept fresh in his small cellar. "Let's have a last one!" he said. He put a bottle of gnole on the table. We drank to health and peace.

"I thank you for your hospitality, and for my men," said officer Albert.

"Good luck to you for the future of mathematics," I answered.

We shook hands. A few minutes later, leaving in complete disorder, the Germans were out of sight. "All is well that ends well." I declared. "I rush to the rectory to deliver the wounded, now that we are sure that they are gone. It was again a close call. Had they been of the tough kind, we were dead. They would have searched everywhere and discovered our wounded. We were lucky with that officer Albert and his bunch of lousy soldiers. I'll be back in a few minutes. Then, I will need a drink to relax."

Michelle was still at the rectory.

"Why did you wait for me?" I asked.

"I wanted to be sure that everything went OK between you and the German officer."

"He was a nice guy. Anyway, you have been wonderful, both my grandmother and you. Let me tell you the incredible part of the story...."

I transported Marc's wounded men to the hospital during the night without any problem. I refused Marc's help because the Citroën was not an appropriate ambulance. It was OK for four people in peacetime, but not five in wartime, one of them with a wounded leg that had to stay as stiff as a piece of lumber. He also accepted the idea of remaining with his men as their commanding officer instead of wandering on the roads.

On another occasion, we "captured" ten German soldiers who had apparently no desire to fight for their lives, but rather to preserve them by not fighting. I was with the "commandant" at his quarters in the woods when one of his men came to give him a message. A group of twelve German soldiers had been sighted some 10 kilometers south, along the railroad tracks. Immediately, the commandant chose twenty men.

"We will surprise them," he told me. "Twenty tough men are plenty enough. Why don't you come with me? I know! You are not supposed to. Come as an observer. You'll do nothing but observe. We'll do the work."

Four cars hit the small road that ran more or less parallel to the railroad. The "commandant" was driving a big, good-looking black American Dodge Sedan. The "commandant" always appeared in cars that nobody else had. The three other cars carried twenty men who were squeezed in them like sardines in cans.

We drove for 6 miles before the "commandant" stopped. The sardines disembarked to look like armed men. Deploy and walk. We were walking for fifteen or twenty minutes when one of the men signaled that "they" were there. He showed the direction with an arm extended like a sign on the side of a road. The "commandant" ordered, also by signs, a turning movement to surround them with the classic order, "Wait for my signal to shoot."

The enemy was not moving. Had it perceived our approach and waited to give us a warm reception? We were unable to figure it out, but it seemed incredible. The circle of our twenty warriors slowly shrank toward its center. No movement. It was even more incredible. Our circle shrank to the point where we were on them. They were effectively twelve men dressed in unusual uniforms. Even more unusual was the fact that they did not move when they understood that they were surrounded. They were lying on their backs in the sun, three of them with a gun at their side. We laughed like crazy. It's always good to have a pretext to laugh when you are at war. We overdid it. They took a sitting position when they heard us laughing.

"We, not soldiers," one of them said, finally getting up. "We, railroad men. No rail-road. No trains." He repeated several times "no trains," before imitating someone walking, walking, lowering his shoulders more and more, and falling on the ground to make us understand that they were dead tired of walking. "Water, please, water!"

"No water," the "commandant" said.

"We, go to Germany, go to Germany," the man said. He had on his sleeves the stripes of a corporal.

"Yes!" the "commandant" said. "After a vacation in our prisoner camp." They were a bunch of old guys who did not want to walk any further. When they all got up, three guns remained on the grass. We had to pick them up.

We never understood how the twelve fit in the Dodge. It must be noted that the corporal went on the front seat with us.

When we reached the "commandant's" quarters, a house in the woods, two of the Germans had almost passed out in the car. There was a water pump in front of the house. The "commandant" stopped next to it. The Germans exited the Dodge. One of our men began pumping. The corporal gave an order. A straight row of Germans formed in front of the pump, the two most miserable in first position, the corporal at the end. He drank last.

"Admirable German discipline!" the "commandant" commented. "They are not even in army uniforms. Those guys are mad!"

After the loss of my pass, I could have adopted the solution of a motorcycle, but we had no motorcycles. They certainly had not been very popular in our area. Those we found were in too bad shape, with no spare parts to fix them. Plus, although a motorcycle can be easily camouflaged, it does not provide much protection in case of a dangerous encounter.

A car was not the ideal either, but the "Traction Avant Citroën" was a popular car. We had a certain number of them. The body of a car provided an eventual protection against bullets, but it was not always easy to get out of the "Traction Avant," whose front doors opened in the direction opposite to the direction of the road. It meant that, instead of being eventually protected by the door acting as a bullet shield, you were directly exposed to enemy fire if the enemy were in front of you, waiting for you, as it usually was.

As I've already said, the "Traction Avant" was also a very popular car with the Gestapo. When sighting that car, Germans never knew if it were one of theirs. Usually, they did not fire first and asked questions afterward.

Once, Marc and I were driving on a straight part of a road when we saw a convoy of six military trucks coming in front of us. The only thing to do was the usual. Do not panic! When your heart stops beating like crazy, keep your hands firm on the wheel, and act as if you were a member of the Gestapo. Do not change speed, beep-beep the horn when passing them, and wave to the soldiers in the trucks. Those Germans never realized that we were not members of the Gestapo.

We just said, "Ouf!"

If the "Traction Avant" was my favorite, I was also, according to circumstances, using other types of cars. That morning, I was driving a brand-new four-door "Matford" sedan. The car was the brainchild of the marriage between the French Mathis and the American Ford. It gave it the look of an American car. It was bigger and heavier than the "Traction Avant". We had borrowed it from a retired old doctor who accepted almost reluctantly a small piece of paper bearing my signature in exchange. He was happy, he said, to contribute modestly to our fight with his car, not being able to contribute physically. The car had been garaged since the beginning of the war, and our mechanics declared that they had had some work to put its seized engine in running condition.

It was running fine on that morning. I had four passengers, one in the front seat and three on the back. Warned of the passage of German units in the area, I was using a road that was only a serpentine dirt path connecting one farm to the next, almost to our final destination of Prince's farm. The four men, more or less carpenters, had been loaned for a few days to Mary to repair a shack that was going to serve as her temporary radio room.

The morning was glorious. It endowed our slow ride with the feeling of a promenade in a quiet landscape. The promenade suddenly ended when we faced on a curve a German sidecar that was hidden from our sight by trees. It was equipped with a machine-gun that fired on us before we could react. A bullet went through the windshield, straight to the forehead of the passenger seated in the middle of the back seat.

In a sudden reaction, I pushed the gas pedal furiously to the floor. The Matford was instantly transformed into a black tank aimed at crushing the sidecar. There was no room for both of us on the dirt road. All went so fast that the gunman did not even try to fire again at us. The sidecar's driver had immediately realized my intention. He made a sharp right turn toward the meadow. Unfortunately for him, a ditch sided the path. The sidecar overturned. I brutally stopped the car. Three of my passengers jumped out of it, firing at the two Germans who were dead before they could get back on their feet and reach for their firearms. Then, a surprising scene took place. As white as a ghost, our hurt passenger came out of the car, carbine in hands. He took it by the barrel, walked to one of the dead Germans. With a powerful swing, he broke it on the helmet worn by the soldier. Then he sat down heavily on the ground and touched his head.

When it is not your time, it is not your time. The bullet, certainly slowed down by going through the windshield, had hit him on top of his forehead but at an angle that deviated it. Instead of penetrating the bone, it moved around it, furrowing around a third of his head before shattering the back window. Skin and hair were replaced by a bloody narrow groove, but his life was not in danger.

I knew that young man, having met him previously. His name had a flavor of Renaissance poetry, Flore, if such was his name. His manners had the sweetness of a nice personage evolving in a tapestry of those foregone times. Afterward, he was unable to explain his violent gesture. Everyone always wondered what had happened to him. He apologized to Prince for destroying the carbine. Prince accepted the apology and gave him another one.

Prince had the two Germans picked up and buried, and he retrieved the sidecar. No traces, no reprisals. As they had been killed, we never learned what those two men were doing on that dirt road in the middle of nowhere. I confessed to Mary how I had been involuntarily involved in a military action. She took her coolest attitude to tell me, "For this time, you are excused, but try not to repeat too often that type of action. I still need you." Then she smiled, "You have been lucky!"

A few days later, I had to go back to Prince. I knew that he needed supplies, because many fights or skirmishes were taking place on the road. Among the prisoners made prior to my salesman like visit of that day was a colonel with a wounded knee. When I arrived, he was sitting on the ground in front of the farm. Unable to walk, he was not guarded. I was surprised when he called me with a gesture of the hand. He did not speak a single word of French. He took out of his jacket a pocketbook and, out of the pocket book, an identification card. I do not remember his name. It came with a "von."

Then, he showed me a photograph. In front of a large house located in what looked like a park, a woman stood with her arms around a girl who was between ten and twelve years old, both with long curled blond hair and a large smile on their faces. The photograph had been shot from too far away to allow a clear vision of their faces. "Very nice," I said stupidly. The colonel moved several times one index finger from the photograph to his chest to make me understand that it was his wife and his daughter. I smiled and gave him back the photograph. He put the card and the photograph back in his jacket, and turned his head away without a word.

A few minutes later, I could see that Prince was having one of his bad days. When he came out of the farmhouse, he had two pieces of paper in his hands. One was his list of supplies. I took it. The other one was a flyer that he read to me, accentuating strongly the words, "Terrorists must be ground like meat in pâté." Before I could take the document from his hands to read it, he exploded. Two of his men had been killed two days ago, and he had found the flyer on the road. He walked to the colonel, put the paper under his nose, tore it into small pieces that he smashed under his shoes, screaming, "And this is what I do with your Hitler!"

Then, he calmed a little. "I am going to execute that man, right now, in front of our prisoners. War reprisals."

I told him that war reprisals did not mean much in the middle of the woods, witnessed by a bunch of defeated Germans, and that, in order to have any value, the reprisal would have to be brought to the knowledge of the whole German army. My call for disguised clemency did not work.

"I need to do that," he insisted, "if it were only for the morale of my men."

I did not see the logic, but Prince was like a furious animal wounded by the death of two of his men. It was no use trying to make him change his mind. I disagreed with Prince, but was unable to intervene. It was neither my role, nor my right. Nor could I leave the farm immediately. My reputation of tough guy and my good relationship with Prince were at stake. One hour later, unable to stand up, the colonel was seated on the ground in front of the prisoners standing in ranks behind the fence. Prince had nominated a delegation of twenty of his men to witness the execution. A firing squad of five men came and stood close to the colonel.

On Prince's instruction, a translator explained to the prisoners the meaning of "meat for pâté" that was the reason for the execution. I had again a problem taking what I was watching for real, but I was in fact in the middle of the woods, with a German officer on his butt who was going to be killed while his wife and his daughter waited for his return, smiling on a photograph somewhere in Germany. The scene would have been more acceptable if the man had made an abject plea for his life instead of displaying a dignified acceptance of his fate. He did not give the Hitler's salute, but remained immobile with his hands on his legs. The seconds before the squad fired lasted for centuries. The German officer fell on his back. The prisoners standing at attention made the German military salute in the silence of death. So much for us!

Alibert checked the man. He was five times dead. Five bullets had ravaged his heart. At such a short distance, the squad could not miss. Somewhere, at the edge of the forest, was a common pit for dead Germans. It would be the colonel's last station. We left when the execution was over, at the exception of Alibert who was in charge of the wounded and the dead, and the four men carrying the body. I managed afterward to approach Alibert and ask him to give me the pocketbook of the colonel during my next visit. I wanted to give it to Mary who, someday, would send it to his wife. He promised. Prince had not retrieved it from the colonel's pocket. It was intact in the side of his jacket that had not been destroyed by the bullets, but too many eyes were still watching.

I was ready to leave when Prince came to the window of my car, "OK! I told him. You get your supplies."

"You understand?" he asked.

"Of course! I understand. Come on! War is war, and you have to do what you have to do."

During my next visit, Melody put the pocketbook in my hand. She had not been allowed by the doctor to watch the execution, but like everybody else, she knew every detail of it. She did not talk about it.

"I have discovered my vocation," she told me. "I want to be a doctor like Doctor Alibert. He is such an example and a wonderful man. After the war, I will study to become a doctor. Doctor Alibert promised me that he would help me."

From that day on, she kissed me on both cheeks.

I visited Prince again several days later with a precise message from Mary. "OK!" I told him. "Here is the situation. According to our latest information, many retreating

German units are now not far from us. They travel slowly east and northeast to try reaching the east of France and Germany. The order from London is that we must try everything in our power to slow them down. Tonight, I will drive to give the 'commandant' the order to move his forces to join yours. Prepare your camp to welcome him and provide him with some basic needs."

"I'll prepare everything. He can come."

I left Prince and drove back with no problem to the mission. I felt almost like a tourist admiring the countryside on a peaceful summer afternoon. I had hoped that Michelle would be at the mission. She was not, but I did not dare to ask about her. Mary introduced a young and decent young man, a college-boy type. "I think that Yves, here, could be your assistant or secretary, if you prefer. He could take care of lots of details for you. See if you can work together. Let me know. Take him with you tonight."

Desire or order, I did not know. I had no need for an "assistant" or a "secretary," but why irritate Mary by arguing? Besides, this young man might effectively be of some help, after all. I waited until sunset to leave again. Michelle did not show up but, while waiting, I began to think that I liked her presence. I missed her when I had not seen her for a while.

I wanted to arrive at the house of the "commandant" at night, by precaution. I was accustomed to driving at night without lights, so long as the night was not completely pitch-black. It was already dark, almost night, when I reached the top of the hill dominating the village. I stopped the car and cut off the engine. A fire in the middle of the village was sparkling in the darkness. In front of us, the road went down in a straight line to the center of the village through Main Street. At the end of Main Street, the road made a right-angled turn. The fire was in that part of the village between the right angle of the road and the farther railroad crossing. After listening attentively and watching for eventual movements in the village, I was uncertain of what was going on, and what I could do. I already knew where the fire was raging. I could see bursts of flames and heavy smoke. "Oh my God!" I thought. Then, I said aloud. "It's his home!"

The "commandant," "la Blouse," was the second person I had to contact after contacting Prince. He was located on the east side of our sector. The Arabian telephone functioned between us, and I finally met him for the first time. "Commandant" was his nickname, but we never called him anything else. He was a man in his forties, all roundness, jovial, but apparently very determined to fight the Germans. He exuded cheerfulness and *joie de vivre*, but also, perhaps, too much insouciance when he was personally concerned.

After our first contact, I was invited several times by the "commandant" and his family. They had a beautiful house, with very valuable paintings. I remembered a small Boudin among them, and also the liquor glasses that bore four lines. The lower line was marked "Ladies;" the line above was marked "Gentlemen," the line above bore the drawing of a small pig, and the upper line the drawing of a fat pig. They had two children, a boy and a girl. The girl was eighteen and charming.

"Forget it!" I thought. "I have to find him. I only hope that the whole family escaped." At the same time, I was wondering how that had happened. With the Germans, you could never know. However, I had a mission to accomplish that made it imperative to find the commandant and ask him to move his men to join Prince's force.

"Let's go!" I told my assistant-secretary.

He looked at me with surprise. "But it's burning," he said. "Shall we not wait?"

"Wait for what?" I did not start the engine. I put the gears in neutral, released the parking brake, and the car began to roll down the slope. Foot on the brake and windows wide open to receive any noise of the German presence, I let the car reach the piazza. Except for the glare and the cracklings of the fire coming from the "commandant's" house, there was no trace of life in the whole village. I stopped the car in the middle of the piazza, and said, "Let's go and see where our people are."

I opened my door while my assistant opened his on the other side, turning on our seats to step down. We did not even have our feet on the ground that a string of machine gun bullets passed over our heads. My mind went at lightning's speed. I even had the time to think that it was becoming one of my specialties to be greeted by a volley of bullets each time I was getting out of a car. The lightning contained a message. "They don't want to kill us, otherwise we would already be dead. They want to catch us alive." Perhaps that was completely wrong. They had only missed.

"Come on, let's go! Run!"

At the same time, the noise of a moving tank came from the street where the house burned. We succeeded in reaching Main Street, out of sight of the Germans. Taken by surprise, they had not reacted fast enough. The tank was moving slowly. It was not yet in Main Street while my assistant and I were running on the right side of the street, pushing doors and widows to find one that would open. Luckily, the tank was still moving cautiously. "They don't move fast enough to catch us alive," I thought. "But how come there is a tank here?"

Finally a low window opened. Without thinking, I grabbed my assistant-secretary by the neck of his shirt and the bottom of his pants and, with a force increased tenfold by a surge of adrenalin, I threw him flying through the open widow. I jumped inside behind him and closed the window.

The tank passed several times in front of the house, but we had disappeared. As soon as we were inside, we went to the back of the house to find a possible exit if we were obliged to run again. Both the kitchen and the family room had a door opening outside on a garden.

I put the light on in the kitchen. The disposition of the rooms made that light invisible from the street. I looked around, "I suppose that all the people fled from their houses when they heard the Germans coming," my assistant said. I suggested that all questions would certainly be answered later. Half the house had been transformed into a pharmacy, but nobody was there. Adjacent to the kitchen was a dining room. The table was formally set for a dinner that was waiting in the kitchen: pan, butter, eggs already beaten in a large bowl, and prepared mushrooms to make an omelet. "They certainly left in a hurry," I commented. Salad, cheese, and fruit were also ready to go.

I lit the gas stove, put the pan on the burner, and started to cook the mushrooms in butter.

"Are you completely crazy?" my assistant asked with anxiety in his voice. "You are not going to prepare a dinner while the Germans are after us?" That was the end of Yves' collaboration with me. This young man had no humor. I was going to give him back to Mary with my thanks.

"The Germans are after us for sure but, so far, they did not find us," I answered, "and they did not start destroying the whole village. If they had seen us dashing into this house, they would have followed us. How they came here without being noticed, we don't know. Are they only a commando unit with not enough troops to destroy the town? We don't know. Plus, think of it, they fired at us when they saw us, but they don't know how many we are. They don't like to fight the resistance during the night, even with their tanks. If they came especially for the 'commandant,' it is because someone betrayed him. They burned only his house. They don't know where we are, you and me, but we know that they are turning in circles outside. So, why not have a dinner that was prepared for us? It will not change the course of history, but it will do us a lot of good. I'll tell you something: my prime reaction to fear is to eat or drink. If, someday, I'm still alive, and I write my memoirs about the resistance, I will talk a lot about food and wine because they were my only way to overcome my fears. The memoirs will show that I was permanently gripped by fear at every turn of the road. I was frightened to death a few minutes ago, not you? I need to eat and drink, now. Let's have dinner! In any case, it's better to die with a full stomach rather than an empty stomach. If we don't see the owners before we leave, we will write them a thank-you note. Anonymously, of course!"

"I am not really hungry," my assistant whispered

"Suit yourself, I eat," I said. "Please, pass that bottle of wine which had time to breathe, as you can see. It was opened for us!"

Finally my assistant could not resist the smell of the mushroom omelet that was too big for me alone, and the temptation of the nice red Bordeaux. After eating, we waited. The tank was no longer passing by. The street was silent, but we kept waiting. After a long while, we heard voices in the street, voices talking in our own language. Under-ground people had resurfaced and the inhabitants were coming back to their village.

We had no more time to thank the pharmacist and his family personally for their dinner. I still had a message to deliver to the "commandant." We went directly to the house that was now a smoking ruin. Four men were standing and talking aloud in front of it. I recognized immediately the man I had to contact. "Commandant," I said, "I have a message for you, but what about your family? I am terribly sorry to see that your house is destroyed. It was a beautiful house and all that was inside was beautiful...."

"It's only a house, René. Thank God, all my family is safe, including me. You met my mother-in-law and you know how strong she is. She insulted the Germans, but they let her go. They are at a friend's house. You will not believe it when I tell you my story. There was no way to fight tanks in the middle of town. They would have destroyed everything." Looking at my assistant, he added, "But why are you here? When did you arrive?"

I told our own story to the "commandant." He found enough grace to laugh. "So, you ate the eggs and drank the wine of Fontenelle?" he said. "I'll thank him for you."

"In any case, you have to tell me your story, 'Commandant'," I said. "I have to give a report to the mission. You have to tell me if you are able to execute the movement that we require from you. You have to move your men immediately to join forces with Prince. Can you do it?"

"Of course, I can. Tell Mary that we are going to move immediately. It's time to tell everyone, pack up the materiel in our trucks, and move at dawn. Let me think. We will make a convoy, a real convoy, with all the trucks and cars. We have enough gas to go."

"Don't worry about gas. They have more than plenty over there. They have the gas tankers that came from you. There is one thing that you must do. That is to paint white crosses on top of all your vehicles. Knowing you, we supposed that you would move immediately. London is aware of your move. You will not risk being attacked by Allied planes if you paint those white crosses on your convoy."

"OK! I know where to find white paint. It does not need to be of prime quality. I still have a full truck of gasoline. If we have an encounter with the Germans, we will fight our way through. Tell Mary that we will be there early in the morning. I have people to help my family. They are absolutely able to survive, even after the loss of our house. But before you go, let me tell you what happened.

"The paintings and the grand piano?"

"Gone in smoke. I should have removed them. I don't know why I didn't do it. I was too confident. But for the railroad, we are so far away from anywhere. A house is only a house. But let me tell you what happened. We had been taken by surprise."

What had happened was that several hours ago, while he was standing alone exactly at the place where he was now, in front of his house, a man in shorts had appeared at the end of the street, coming from the direction of the railroad crossing. A man in shorts with a gun was not an extraordinary sight in a village that was supposedly devoted to the resistance. The only difference was that the man shouted at him before firing at him and missing him. The "commandant" realized that the man in shorts was a German who shouted in German.

The "commandant" could not understand how that man could be there. His men had put down a series of the railroad's electrified pylons. They were lying across the tracks to stop any possible traffic. No German convoy had been signaled. The "commandant" overlooked the fact that the Germans had succeeded, with an armored train carrying three tanks, at forcing their way through the pylons in record time. It was an operation impossible for a normal train, but not for an armored train pulled by two specially equipped locomotives. What confused the commandant was the fact that the man was in shorts instead of wearing an army uniform, whatever it would be. The "commandant" ignored that the man was effectively in uniform, since the uniform of the Africa Corps, back from North Africa included shorts

But the man was there, followed by a tank. Before he could recover from his surprise, the commandant was running on a narrow path that opened across the street in front of him. It ended up on a wire-latticed fence too high to jump over. When fear does not paralyze, it can, on the contrary, give wings. The "commandant" literally flew over the fence, unable to explain afterward how he did it. The German fired at him, but missed again. Finally, the "commandant" found himself in a cul-de-sac with no exit but two doors in front of him. The left one was closed. The right door opened to a charming and odoriferous "cabinet de champagne", a wooden seat between two walls with a hole in the middle and a lid over the hole. A grenade in one hand for an eventual last stand, the commandant told me that he had seriously considered taking a bath in what you can imagine, had his follower come to the cul-de-sac. The German did not come. He stopped in front of the wire-latticed fence.

At dawn, the "commandant" made his move. A whole convoy of vehicles hit the road in the direction of Prince. A big white cross was displayed on the roofs of the vehicles. All his men were very excited. They were "armed to the teeth," and ready, if necessary, to confront the Germans, but nothing happened. According to the "commandant," it was a military promenade. Only music was missing. I believe that he would have loved being preceded by a fanfare, just for the sake of provoking the Germans. He had, now, a personal score to settle with them.

Prince had no knowledge of the burning of the "commandant's" house. When he heard about it from the "commandant," he went wilder than the "commandant" had ever been. The "commandant" appreciated, and they drank together to the revenge they were going to extract from the Germans.

The depth of the forest, the large farm, and the fields behind it surprised the "commandant." A large and long green meadow extended between the forest and the farm's buildings. One of the very first thoughts of the "commandant" concentrated on that meadow. He considered it with great attention before declaring to Prince that they were going to get "it."

"Get what?" Prince asked.

"It! The plane."

"The plane?"

"This piece of meadow is sufficient for a small plane to land on and take off. You may not know it, but I fly. I have a plane, but it is too far away... if it still exists. In fact, I don't know if it still exists because I don't dare to go where it is and find out. But I know where there is another plane. It belongs to one of my friends who disappeared at the beginning of the war. The plane is in a barn, 20 kilometers from here. We can go and retrieve it. You said that you have two good mechanics. They will put it back in flying condition. An engine is an engine!"

"What for?"

"What do you mean, what for? Think! Number one, we have a plane for observation of any movement by the Germans on the roads around here. Number two, we can fly in the pattern of the small German spy plane. What the Germans do not know is that the small plane I am talking about is a fast little biplane equipped for aerobatics. Aerobatics was its job before the war at popular country festivals. It can make fun of the no fun German plane. They will be very upset."

"Will you fly it yourself?" Prince asked with some anxiety.

"Oh, no! I have to take care of my men. But I have the man to fly it."

"In that case, let's do it. We will be the first and only underground group with an eye in the sky. Let's study the technicalities."

The plane was in a barn. It was an occasion to use the expression "in the middle of nowhere." Two pickup trucks left at night with the two German mechanics and ten armed men in the trucks, Prince, the future pilot, and I in the Dodge driven without hesitation by the "commandant." He knew where he was going and, around midnight, we were in front of the barn. When the two rolling doors opened, the plane appeared, a two-seater yellow machine with bright red stripes artistically featured. A real camouflage for a warplane!

The ten men took position around the barn. "To work!" commanded the "commandant."

The plan consisted of dismantling the wings in the light provided by one of the trucks. The wings would be transported on one of the trucks while the body of the plane, with tail on the other truck and wheels on the road, would follow. The project was completed in three hours. The two mechanics did wonders. There were lots of hands available, and the convoy took the road back to the farm without incident. We were using only small winding roads that jumped over two little brooks with the help of small bridges. Our car was leading the way. All of a sudden, the "commandant" stopped. The "commandant," followed by Prince, jumped out of the car, passed in front of the hood, and remained immobile for a few seconds before coming back to us.

"The dirty son of a bitch!" Prince said. "That son-of-a-bitch Charles, blew up the bridge. I don't know what kind of a war the communists wage, but they never collaborate. That bridge represents nothing. No German will ever use this road. Or, perhaps, he did it on purpose if he knew that we were here. How could he have known that? I will have to settle that with him soon. I cannot stand him. He is a nuisance. But that does not solve our problem. We cannot back up and make a U-turn. We don't even have the room for it. Listen, 'commandant!' Look! They do such a lousy job that they are not even able to blow a bridge correctly! Look at the gap! Not even the width of a bar or a coffee table!"

"A coffee table? You are a genius, Prince!" The "commandant" exulted. "You are a genius!" he repeated to Prince's astonishment. "Yes, this is the solution: coffee tables to fill the gap and replace the bridge. The cut is clean, and right in the middle. Two tables will be enough. Come on! Two kilometers away, there is a small café. I know it because I came here several times with my friend to check his plane before he left France for America. We go over there, we borrow two tables, and we pass. We take four of our boys to carry the tables. We walk. It's no more than a twenty-minute walk."

The café owner was a joyous man who got up without protesting. He seemed to enjoy the situation and was happy to help us. "I'll go with you. I want to keep an eye on my tables," he declared. "How many tables do you need?

Two sturdy tables were enough to cover the missing part of the bridge. They supported easily the weight of the two trucks. We brought the tables back to the café. It was now four-thirty in the morning. It was time to go. Dawn was not far away. We had a fast one with the café's owner, who would have been very offended if we had not accepted. We had to promise that we would come back for a real one when things got better. One hour later, we were at Prince's headquarters.

"We are going to put your mechanics to work right away," the "commandant" declared. "Feed them well. The plane must fly soon. It seems to be in perfect shape, but for the fact that the engine has not turned for several years. The tires did not suffer too much on the road. They are still good enough. They will be OK on the grass here. Right now, that plane is as visible as the sun in the middle of the day. We are going to repaint it, decorate it with three-colored cockades, and name it "RES 1" for Resistance One. We now have our own air force! We will give an automatic rifle to the passenger in case they meet with the German who flies again. The German plane is not armed. Looks a little like World War I, but we are talking about slow planes at low altitudes. I considered many times firing at the German when he flew by, touching the top of the trees, but it was too risky."

A week later, the plane made its first test flight. The plane brought several times useful information that allowed us to prepare a welcome committee for the convoys that passed on "the road." The combined forces of Prince and the "commandant" attacked everything that moved. When trucks carried soldiers, the exchanges of fire were sometimes very violent. Single trucks passing at full speed usually escaped, even if they suffered from wounded or dead on board in doing so. Grouped trucks in convoys traveled more slowly. They were subjected to a barrage of fire by a line of men camouflaged on the side of the road.

Prince adopted a method that the "commandant" had recommended. Rather than taking prisoners or inheriting wounded, their men retreated to the woods, leaving to the Germans the care of picking up their wounded or dead, and letting them drive away. Wounded prisoners and prisoners were a bad bargain. Wounded had to be taken care of, and medical or surgery supplies were scarce. The hospital staff was doctor Alibert and his nurses, but it was too much for them in difficult conditions, or if the wounds were too severe. The prisoners had to be fed and it was a burden. The prisoners' camp was very simple: a fence in the woods. Escape was not in the minds of most prisoners; to go where? Prince managed to give them decent food. Even if comfort was missing, the war was over for them. Of course, the noise of war was still very close. They could hear the fights on the road and, once in a while, one or two prisoners joined them.

Disabled trucks were towed into the forest to erase all traces of fighting that could alert oncoming Germans. On three occasions, the fights on the road took on an aspect of trench warfare with Prince and the "commandant" bringing in reinforcements to lead a veritable charge against a stopped convoy. Such action took several lives on both sides. One of them ended when the Germans surrendered, two others when the attackers disappeared into the woods, leaving demoralized Germans to run away after putting their dead and wounded in their trucks. According to the road they chose, the same reception awaited them at the corner of Marc's "woods."

Mary was waiting for me.

"We have a problem," she said.

"Do we?"

"Kind of."

Mary put a piece of paper under my eyes.

"And what is that?" I asked after a glance at the list on the paper.

"It's ammunition for a thousand people. According to my information, there are no more than one hundred in the woods. You are also aware that they never coordinate their movements with ours. I would like you to go and see the so-called Colonel Charles to find out what that means. You can make any decision you want. I will cover you but, before giving him anything, we must know how many men he has. I mean an exact number. Otherwise, he will have nothing, not one single bullet. That is my order."

"Clear enough. When do you want me to go?"

"No rush, but as soon as possible. We still have three days before sending our requests to London. Give me an answer in the meantime."

"I will go tomorrow. Are they still at the same location?"

"Apparently, yes. Be here at ten. We will synchronize our movements. You will go but, if you are not back at a time we will set, we will get you out. I don't trust Charles at all."

I knew where the communist group was located. I nevertheless made a mistake and had a problem making a U-turn in the woods. I succeeded after much maneuvering. "They are somewhere around. I'll try every path. They'll find me, or I'll find them."

I was now on the right path. I had hardly entered in the woods when two rifles' nozzles showed their ugly apertures on my windshield. "British mission for Colonel Charles," I said.

"You leave the car here. We will accompany you."

We walked for ten minutes before arriving in a glade in the middle of the woods. For whatever reason, no trees had grown there. A dozen tents made of sturdy material formed the camp. They were spread in a half-circle and camouflaged under the trees.

The first time I visited him, Colonel Charles was seated at a table that stood right in the middle of the glade. He was in his early fifties, dressed in some kind of fatigue uniform. His hair was a half-inch long and stood straight up. He displayed the martial air of a conqueror or a dictator, reminding me of Mussolini. "He is performing his role on stage," I thought. "I suppose that he wants to impress me."

"Colonel Charles, I presume," I said.

171

"I am not Doctor Livingston," answered Colonel Charles with a smile.

The "I presume" was too much. I had been stupid. Colonel Charles added, "You belong to the British mission, if I understand correctly. Then, you are the man I need to talk to. We have a problem. As you know, we have proceeded to perform a certain number of operations against the Germans. We need supplies."

I had already supplied him with enough armament for one hundred men. Today, he was asking for one thousand. I did not go directly to the heart of the problem.

"Before we talk supplies," I said, "explain to me why you do not cooperate more closely with us. You are certainly aware of the problem you created one night when you blew up a bridge that we were using to come back to our base. Why did you do it?"

"With the plane? You have a nice little toy. I swear to you that I didn't do it on purpose. Bad coincidence!"

"You can use irony," I said. "That plane is very useful in the detection of German convoys. But that is not why I am here. We could be much more efficient if you were more cooperative."

"Let me tell you something, my young friend. Here we are people who have faith in communism, and we prepare ourselves for the after war realities. The end of the war will see the triumph of communism. In other words, you are waging your war; we are waging ours. They are not the same. We fight the Germans because they are our enemies, but we will not cooperate with you because, in some ways, you are also our enemy, our bourgeois enemy."

"Forget the politics," I said, angered by his speech. "You can say what you want, you depend on us to wage 'your' war."

"Yes, but what we do, you don't have to do. That's why we need some supplies."

"I have your list. Here it is. You are asking for guns and ammunition for a thousand people. Where are they? If I judge by what I see here, you are still no more than a hundred men."

"That's right. We are one hundred and six to be correct. The rest of our people are country people in the farms that you see around, in several villages, and two towns. They are ready to go. I can give you names and locations."

I was trying to think fast.

"You mean that they are not fighters. They are civilians that you want to arm; for what, if they are not here with you? You want an armed militia that will take over the country after the liberation, and you count on us to arm it."

I paused. "You want to repeat the Bolshevik revolution in France," I said after several seconds of silence. "I am afraid that I can provide you with supplies only for the men that you have here, one hundred and six, and you have to give me your actual stock of arms and ammunition. I know that you will cheat, but we have the record of what we gave you previously."

Colonel Charles' face lost its smile. He looked behind me. I immediately felt that the two ugly gun nozzles were applied, this time, on my back at the level of my belt. In a new gust of anger, I said, "If that is the way you make the revolution, you lose."

I looked at my watch. "If I am not back in, let say, exactly twenty eight minutes, they'll come to pick me up. You are one hundred… and six…. They are one thousand."

"Let him go."

"It was a pleasure talking with you, Colonel," I said. "Plus, it was very interesting to learn your real intentions from your own mouth. We will be on our guard when we come out of the woods. In the meantime, we will provide you with some supplies."

Back to the mission, I reported word for word my exchange with the so-called Colonel Charles. Everyone agreed that it meant only one thing. When the time comes to exit the woods, all our forces will have to be ready to interfere when the communists will try to seize municipal buildings, post offices, and so on. Ready to fight if necessary. "We are going to give precise instructions to all our commanders," Mary said. "The communists are able to try a *coup de force*. We will provide Charles with some ammunition to have a clear conscience if he is attacked. Again, you never can tell. But he has enough guns already. They are not fighting. What have they done, with the exception of blowing a few bridges on roads that are never used by the Germans? As you said, they are not fighting our war but theirs. We will not help them."

"Michelle," I said, "I need you. I am sorry, but I want you to go and see dear doctor Duprieux to ask him if he can provide my friend Alibert with what he needs for his hospital, or tell us where we can find the items on his list. Arrange for a meeting between the doctor and me. I will walk with you to the Three Points. Take your bicycle. You'll go from there to the doctor. I will leave you there to get my car back."

We walked almost silently as if we were aware of each other's thoughts, and did not want to start unveiling them. At least, such was my feeling. The few words we exchanged were only banalities. I had hoped that the walk, that I had no reason to make, would be an occasion for talking, but, so far, it was not. I was more and more attracted to Michelle, even if contradictory feelings still agitated my soul. It was a deep natural impulse, an undefined but strong need for instants of feminine presence in my life, maybe as purely instinctive, as when I put my arm around the shoulder of the woman in the train, or took the so-called Marika in my arms.

While walking, my ears remained, nevertheless, attentive, my eyes looking all around. As we attained the top of a small hill, I saw the first of them at the bottom of the road.

"Get down!" I ordered.

Michelle had seen them. She dropped her bicycle on the grass and we went flat on our bellies. Protected by tall grass, we were invisible from the road. A detachment of Germans, every one of them pushing a bicycle, was walking up the hill. From where we were, we could see that many bicycles did not have tires but rags tied on the wheels with wires. I put my arm on Michelle's shoulders. She did not move.

"Let's count them," I said. "I doubt that they will go very far with their bicycles, but they will be gone before we can alert any of our people. Forty nine, fifty!"

My hand was now on Michelle's waist. She turned to lay on her back, my hand still on her, and now on her abdomen. She took my hand and pulled me toward her.

"Kiss me," she said.

"But you are the country girl who does not want to hear about city boys!"

"Don't talk! Kiss me. You always talk too much!"

"Michelle...," I started. But I was so close to her that I put my lips on hers. Suddenly, I hoped for more, but she said, "No! Not now, not here! Come tomorrow at three in the afternoon in the little barn at the end of P'tit Louis' farm. I will wait for you. If you do not come tomorrow, I will wait for you the day after tomorrow."

I was so surprised that I remained silent.

"Did you lose your tongue again?" she asked. "Or are you so surprised that you don't know what to say?"

I would have beaten myself for being so slow.

"Kiss me again," she said. "It may help you to make a decision."

I kissed her. "You know very well that I will come," I said. Then, I became myself again, "But promise me," I added seriously, "that you will be very prudent. You can see that they are still everywhere, and I don't want to lose you."

"I know my way around."

"I know that you know your way around, but be very prudent, anyway!"

"I'll be... for the love of you. I will go back to the mission and stay there for the night."

"I will spend the night at my grandmother's. Go now, and be careful!"

But the next day, I was at Marc's. Michelle knew that I was not coming to the barn. In the middle of the night, she had knocked at my grandmother's door to give me the information.

"And you are not participating. Mary told me to tell you that it is an order."

"Of course!" I said. "I am not participating. I am never participating, but I will wait until the operation is over."

"I know! I will wait myself for you tomorrow, at the barn. Be prudent. I do not trust you completely, but I don't want to ask you to swear that you will not participate despite Mary's order. I am beginning to know you."

I rushed to the barn of Marc's grandparents where my car was hidden. I drove with no problem to Marc's.

"You are the closest," I told him. "Mary gave her OK. It's a risky operation, but, if her information is correct, there are three hundred "Tirailleurs Sénégalais" war prisoners in ten boxcars. The train had stopped for the night. It has not moved yet."

The Tirailleurs Sénégalais were black soldiers from

Senegal who constituted a regiment in the French army. We could assume that they were being transported to Germany. That would be their death. The train was a twenty-five-boxcar train, old French boxcars of the square type with the inscription, "Men, 40 - Horses, 8." The other cars were regular merchandise cars, meaning that they transported merchandise, not soldiers. The guard was weak, no more than twenty men. The convoy was still 60 kilometers away, running very slowly. It had to let more urgent trains pass it at some stations. The train should be in the afternoon at the site that, Marc and I had agreed on, was definitely the best one to stop it.

"We do not have too much time in front of us," I said.

"Us? I thought you were not participating in operations."

"I am not, but I need a break. I will be an unarmed observer. Mary is going to scream after me, but nobody is obliged to tell her. Now, let's organize."

Marc and I decided that the only way to stop the train was not to blow up the tracks, which would immediately put the Germans on defensive, but to have a supposedly disabled truck in the middle of the tracks at the unguarded crossing with the dirt road that we were going to use to go over there. We hoped that everything would go "swell," with no other German convoy, full of soldiers, following too closely.

Marc had two trucks camouflaged in the woods. We would take both of them to transport our men, and turn one around, close to the tracks, so that it would be able to leave in the right direction in case of emergency. Bushes and trees provided enough concealment for that truck and the men. The other truck had to come out of the woods where it would hide until the last minute. After the operation, it would have to make a U-turn almost on the tracks, difficult but possible. If everything went well, we would have to walk 15 kilometers to go back to Marc's quarters. We ignored the condition of the prisoners. The trucks would eventually be used to transport some of them.

We would place two automatic rifles behind the truck to protect Marc. Our forty men would hide on both sides of the tracks with carbines, Stens, grenades, and handguns. It was necessary to cover both sides, as we did not know on which side the cars' doors opened. We did not want to give the Germans one side of the tracks to fight back. On the forest side, hiding was easy. On the other side, with Eugene in charge, it was more difficult, but there were enough bushes to ensure the effect of surprise. German guards would certainly ride, as usual, on the roofs of the cars and on the front of the locomotive.

The truck would cross the rails when the locomotive would come into sight, break down in the middle of the tracks, and the driver play a panicked man. Marc would be the actor. He would be protected from the fire of the soldiers on the locomotive by the body of the truck. The two automatic rifles, well located in his back to cover him, would open fire on the guards just before the train stopped. We supposed that running slowly, and seeing the truck from far enough away, the engineer would have plenty of time to stop the train close to the truck before pushing it off the tracks with his locomotive.

For once, everything went smoothly. No other convoy was following "ours." Marc performed his role to perfection. The engineer read our minds and came to stop very close to the "disabled" truck. The three soldiers standing on the front of the locomotive were out of combat before they could fire or jump down. There was intense fire from both sides of the cars. Two soldiers fell from the top of the cars. Unexpectedly, the others threw their guns down on the order of one of them. When on the ground, they put their hands up.

"Their guns!" shouted Marc, "and open the cars."

Three hundred black men flowed down from the cars in between the two tracks. They had understood what was going on when they heard the attacking party speaking French. With a big smile, they gave a hand at disarming the Germans. Under the menace of guns, the engineer and his fireman had also stepped down from their locomotive and put their hands on their heads. They were far enough from the Germans not to be heard when they spoke.

"We are French," the engineer said.

"Keep your hands on your heads," Marc answered. "We are making you officially prisoners in front of the Germans. We'll talk later."

Eugene and his men had come back from the other side. "There are two dead on the other side," Eugene said. "Those who fell from the cars. There are also the three in front of the locomotive. We checked. They are definitively dead. We aligned them on the track in front of the locomotive."

"I am sorry," Marc said, "but we can do nothing for them. They will be picked up, you can be sure. And no prisoners!".

"Isn't that a little excessive?" Eugene asked, anxiously. "There are twelve of them."

"Come on, Eugene! I don't mean what you think. I mean that we don't take them, except if you want to guard and feed them personally. We let them go after taking one precaution. Belts and shoes!" Marc shouted.

In a few seconds, three hundred laughing Sénégalais humiliated a small fraction of the German army. Belts and shoes were thrown in Marc's truck. The Germans had to use their hands to keep their pants on and, without shoes, walk on the wooden beams of the track, "walking on eggs," as Frenchies would say. Eugene had some of his men pushing them at the end of the train where they were told to get lost.

Then, a formidable burst of laughter exploded. Years of captivity had not killed the spirit of the Sénégalais.

"What about you?" Marc asked the engineer and his fireman. "Do you want to come with us? The Germans saw that we captured you. That may save you if you want to go back."

"We did not volunteer. We were requisitioned. The Germans are in trouble, but it is not easy to sabotage the railroad. They have killed many of our railroad people and many were blown up by Allied airplanes, or killed by bombings on railroad stations. I don't know about you, Georges, but I don't go back. I bet you that they will accuse us of having worked in collusion with the terrorists. I am officially your prisoner."

"Me, too," Georges said. "I am officially your prisoner. The fire will be dead before they arrive here. They will have to reheat the 'loco' to move it, or bring another 'loco' to pull this one. But don't destroy it! Locomotives are our babies. We will need the remaining ones when the Germans will be gone, if the Allies do not destroy all of them in the meantime."

"OK," Marc said. "We will not touch the train, but we have already lost too much time. Let's get out of here!"

Marc ran to the truck still in the middle of the tracks. There was enough room on the other side to allow him to make a U-turn. He crossed the tracks again. All the German guns had been placed in the other truck. The Sénégalais were not in their best physical shape, but none of them boarded the trucks. We asked the engineer and his fireman to keep company with the truck drivers.

There were only few points that could be dangerous on our way back. We had now a column of three hundred and forty men with our trucks at the end of it. Marc and I were scouting ahead to make sure that the way was clear. Three hours later, we were at Marc's quarters. The black men fell on the ground.

"Well done!" I told Marc. "But now you have a big, big problem on your hands. They are starving, and they will be starving again tomorrow"

"I know! I have to drive one of my trucks again to go to some friendly farms. They will have to wait until the night is dark enough. I believe they are used to waiting. A little more or a little less, they will survive. I will do my best, but I have to get organized for a daily problem. The area has plenty enough to feed everyone here. It only needs some organization."

"Anyway, be prudent with friendly farms. Never can tell, even now! Oh! I know! I will ask P'tit Louis to sell us one of his cows. I will pay him well. He will be very happy to get the money and get rid of one of them. We will help him to kill and quarter it. We can use his barn. We'll do that tomorrow afternoon. After that, you are on your own. I'll give you the money. Maybe your grandfather would also be happy to sell us a cow or two?"

"Go! See you tomorrow! And I will not report your deplorable lack of discipline to anyone."

I reported it myself to Mary. She would learn of it one way or another. She would accuse me of being a liar, dissimulator, with vile mind who had not the courage to recognize his wrongdoings and would use a lot of correct British adjectives borrowed from Kipling and others.

"Do you have an excuse?"

"I needed a break, and I knew many of those men. If you remember I created that group. They were happy to see me going with them!"

"That's not an excuse!"

"I was an unarmed observer!"

"That's even less of an excuse." I saw that she was really angry. She almost screamed, "Swear that you will never do anything like that again," she said. "Mon petit René," she added, and she never addressed me with such a "Mon petit René" before, "you are not expendable. Nobody is indispensable, not even you... but in some ways you are indispensable. Nobody knows better than you the whole underground, and losing you would be a disaster for me!"

Her anger abated. I remained mute in an attitude of fake contrition. She was no dupe. "Don't play that with me," she said. "I know that you have absolutely no remorse for your disobedience, but you have to understand something. The condition of your membership in the mission is that you do not participate in actions with the underground people. You forget that you belong to an artillery regiment of Her Gracious Majesty, and have to conduct yourself as a soldier of that regiment, executing your orders as you receive them, and I give you an order now: you participate in nothing unless under my strict order. Understood?"

She was more British than ever.

"Yes, Sir!" I answered.

She smiled. "I am sorry," she said. "I know that you never trained in your regiment, that you are not a real soldier and want to make an artistic rather than a military career, but you are my responsibility, and I don't want to lose you. I still need you."

It was my turn to say that I was sorry.

She smiled again. "I was talking as your commanding officer," she said. "Now, I talk as your friend, and I don't want to lose you.... Now, back to business! We have to talk a little about the new situation at your friend Marc's quarters."

"I solved the situation for tomorrow," I said. "I have to go to P'tit Louis tomorrow afternoon to let him know that I bought one of his cows. Marc will take care of the rest."

"You always have an answer for everything," Mary said. "It never occurs to you that you may be wrong once in a while?'

I left Marc and three of his men in the company of P'tit Louis and the cow. P'tit Louis was happy to exchange his cow for cash money that Annette needed for the farm, and I did not argue about the price of a pound of beef. I paid him generously and, then, told everyone that I had to go. I had driven Marc and his men in my car. They would go back on foot to their quarters, and would come at night with one of his trucks to pick up the pieces of the cow.

I left and went directly to hide the car in the barn at Marc's grandparents. In fact, nobody ever asked me questions or was surprised to see me coming or going. I left the barn on foot and, without stopping at my grandmother's, turned around the village to arrive at P'tit Louis' small barn from the back.

The barn was a wooden structure housing some of P'tit Louis' machinery when he was working in the fields and some hay that he was gathering on a small parcel behind the barn. Michelle was there, inside, sitting on a blanket stretched on the hay. She did not get up.

"Come here," she said. "Come close to me." With the same simplicity she had showed me her panties when crossing the river, she started unbuttoning her robe that was made in one piece buttoned in front from top to bottom.

"Undress," she softly said. "Please, do it!" she added as she saw me hesitating.

While I was undressing, she came out of her dress and put it on her side. I came close to her. She smiled, "You may have had other girls before me. What about the German woman? Did you make love with her?"

"Are you crazy? She was a deadly snake."

"Would you have otherwise?"

"Would you be jealous?"

"Like a tiger!"

She opened her arms.

"You are the first one," she whispered.

There was a silence and an immobility of both of us that seemed to last for a delectable eternity. "I dare to love against God Himself," I told myself. That was what Samson sings when succumbing to the charm of Delilah. I had seen the opera with my father and had loved it, remembering the words. She was no Delilah and I was no Samson, but all that made my dedication to Christian principles through my family and my education so far overturned into another world. I was going to commit a capital sin: love without God's benediction, but I drowned with no remorse in the immense sea of her green eyes. She was beautiful, and we were lying on virgin sand that no feet had ever spoiled and that will keep forever the imprint of our two bodies. All of a sudden I desperately wanted her, needed her to persuade me that we were for real and that love still existed.

With the grace of nature, we found the gestures of love, and we vanished for a while from the surface of the earth. When she put her head on my shoulder, she said, "It's the war, René. We don't even know if we will be alive tomorrow, and if I die, I will have known love before dying."

That damned war was enough to make the farthest stars cry at the edge of the universe. She had an extraordinary ability to say the most extraordinary things as if they were the most normal or natural things on earth. She was still ahead of me. I had again the sense that she was much more mature than I was. She was a true woman. She made me feel like a lingering kid that war itself had not yet led to puberty. But, after making love with her, I was no longer a child, and that damned war was enough to make the farthest stars cry at the edge of the universe. I was absolutely overthrown by emotion, realizing that I had become one with that woman and that I wanted to keep her for the rest of my life. But, as she had already done once, she put a finger on my lips.

"Don't talk," she said. "I wanted to keep myself for the man who would be my husband, and I did not even ask you if you wanted to be my husband. I did not want to love you. But I love you despite myself. Don't worry! I am responsible for what happened. I asked you. I only hope that you love me a little and will remember me when you will meet a girl from the city."

"There will be no girl from the city. You are my girl from the country, and I love you, and I will always love you."

She did not answer and remained silent during a few seconds. Then, she added unexpectedly, "But I am sure that you have to go somewhere to meet someone who needs something. It's you! You are like that. You always go somewhere to take care of some-thing! Even Mary asks you sometime, 'Where were you?' And you always have a good answer. You were taking care of this or taking care of that. I know, René! I am sure that you have to go. Kiss me, and go! You must go! I will always be there if you want me to be with you."

I went without turning my head. I did not want to see her crying but from that minute, Michelle took total possession of my mind, and painting retrograded to second place in my future priorities.

When I arrived the next morning at the mission, Michelle was there, but Mary did not give me any time for friendly talk. "Our business will wait a little longer," she said. "I just learned that there is a wounded man, three kilometers down from here, on the side of the road where there is a grove. You know where it is. I was waiting for you. Can you go and see about him? If the man is transportable, bring him back here. Be very, very careful. It's a kid who came to tell us. He said that his mother heard some firing from the farm where they live. He said that there is a man on the ground just at the corner of the grove. Please, be careful! It may be a trap!"

"How did that kid know that you were here?" I asked.

"Secret of Polichinelle, as you may say. It's a friendly farm. Don't ask questions. Hurry up!"

"I'll go with you," Michelle said. "I'll give you a hand."

Michelle at my side, I started the engine and drove slowly on the driveway.

"Michelle," I said after we reached the road, "I love you, and I don't want to be separated from you."

There was a short silence.

"Are you proposing?" she finally asked.

She was looking at me and I turned my eyes off the road to look at her.

"Yes, I am," I said. "I want you to be my wife."

"You want to be an artist and I will be a burden for you."

"No darling! On the contrary you will help me by being with me. I know that you are not the farm girl that you pretend to be. You will tell me the truth someday."

"I will, but not today. We don't have time for the history of the whole family. And I am sure that your name is not René, but I will keep on calling you René until you marry me."

"OK! I like it, and I will keep calling you Michelle if such is or is not your name. I can only promise you that there will not be ortolans or Russian caviar every day on the table."

"I need no ortolans or Russian caviar! I believe that nothing could be worse than the incertitude in which we are living every day. I hate that war. After the war everything will seem wonderful."

Three kilometers are a short distance when driving and talking. We were not far from the grove.

"You did not answer me," I said.

"Of course, I say yes! Yes! Yes! Yes!"

I looked at her. Happiness was showing all over her face, but I had to look back at the side of the road. We had passed the grove. At the end of it was an open field. The man was lying on the grass. Michelle and I saw him at the same time. I stopped the car. We rushed to him.

Michelle and I kneeled at his side, Michelle on the other side of the body and facing me. The man on the ground was a young man in his twenties, dressed as a town boy, with the shoes of a town boy, and several wounds on his chest. I wondered what he was doing there in the morning, and who could have killed him. Only Germans. Where were they? Or were they still there?

"He is dead," Michelle said.

He was dead but not presenting the frigidity of death.

"Don't move!" I imperatively told Michelle. She glanced interrogatively at me. "Don't move! I am sure that they are still around." Talking with Michelle and then with my attention suddenly engrossed in finding the man and rushing to him, I had not taken the elementary precaution of inspecting the surrounding carefully, and especially the other side of the road before getting out of the car.

Better, I should have stopped the car and taken it off the road before reaching the grove and then crossing the grove on foot to find out if we were falling into a trap. From where we were and looking in front of us, it was certain that there was nobody, no Germans in the grove, otherwise we would have been already dead, but what about our back? Maybe we were still protected by the body of the car as long as we remained kneeling? If there were Germans on the other side of the road, they might have killed this young man and now were waiting, using him as bait. If they were there, they had seen the kid and let him go on purpose to pick up or kill those who would come to take care of the body.

Maybe were they waiting to see if more than the two of us would show up, otherwise they would have killed me when I came out of the car on their side of the road? In any case, two young people in a car, coming to the rescue of a wounded man on the side of a road, could only be terrorists. If there were Germans on the other side of the road, we had fallen into a trap. If we were still protected by the car, they would shoot at us when we got up. In any case, we could not stay there waiting for them to come after us. I did not even have a weapon. I looked at Michelle.

"When I say 'run' don't question. Run as fast as you can to the woods. If they wait for us to get up, it's our only chance."

I saw that she understood and prepared to run. I hold my breath and said, "run!" At the same time, I got up and started to run. She did the same, and started to run, just on my heels. I put all I had into the dash and I could sense that she was doing the same. Of course, as soon as we got up, we heard the whistling sound of bullets around our ears. Strangely enough, you don't hear the shots but the bullets. We reached the woods and kept on running until we heard nothing other than the noise of crushed dead leaves and small branches under our feet.

"We lost them," I shouted. "We lost them." I turned to look at Michelle. She was on the ground, two or three hundred feet behind me, sitting, her legs folded under her. "What's wrong?" The words came automatically out of my mouth. At the sight of her, a striking pain gripped my stomach. I knew. In a fraction of a second, I was close to her, just in time to take her in my arms as she was falling on her back. Two moist red spots were spreading on her blouse under her breast.

"It's nothing," she said. "I am shot but it's nothing." Her breath was short. "Talk to me." Her eyes were greener and deeper, and her face more beautiful than I had ever thought. "Talk to me," she said again. "Tell me that I am your wife." She had difficulty talking but, after a short while, she added, "Tell me again that you love me."

I was submerged by violent emotions oscillating between pity and love for her, and fury against the Germans. I said, making my voice as gentle as I could, "You know that I have always loved you. I loved you from the very first day I saw you, and I want you for my wife."

There was short silence.

"Kiss me," she said.

My lips, my mouth joined hers and I kissed her gently, avoiding moving her. Incongruously, as in a flash, it reminded me of a Western I had watched a few years before. Dying from a gun shot at the end of the movie, she asks him to kiss her. I chased the thought with anger. My soul was full of furious sentiments of love, despair, and wrath against such a stupid death. I knew that she was dying.

"Michelle, I will marry you," I said, and I would have done it at the moment if it had been possible. I saw that she wanted to answer me. "Don't talk!" I said. "I'll run for help."

"No!" Stay with me!" Her voice was fading. Her blouse was now full of blood. "Stay with me, my love.... With me," she said again. "It's no use, René. Tell me again that you.... Oh, my God!"

She did not say one more word. She remained silent, forever. I was devastated. All of a sudden, the rest of the world vanished. There was no war, no Germans, no men, nobody. We were alone in an unlimited white space. I was desperately in love with her. Her eyes were greener and deeper than I had ever seen them but, now, they were immobile. Her lips had the warmth and softness of life. I left mine on hers for a long period of time.

Then, I came back on earth, an earth where even the innocents were sacrificed. I closed her eyes and fury invaded me again. I could not believe that Michelle, innocent Michelle, my wonderful Michelle was now lying dead on the ground in front of me on the brown leaves of last fall. You don't die when you are twenty years old, when you are loved, when the rays of the sun play at becoming shadows through the leaves of the trees, and when a blackbird sings above your head.

"I must go to the farm and tell the kid's mother not to let her son go into the field at the end of the woods where a dead young man is lying, or in the wood where a dead young woman named Michelle is lying. I must run to Mary, and tell her to move away because she is too close to a road that Germans still use to kill. I must find help to bring Michelle's body and that young man's body to the village."

Everyone in Marc's group knew Michelle. Everyone had seen her joining the group when they gathered in the woods, or when she was coming to contact separately the members of the old group. Almost instantly they heard of what had happened, the unexpected encounter with Germans and her death. When I reached his farm, farmer Georges volunteered immediately to pick up her body with his son and me. We would also pick up the unknown young man and bring both back to Georges' farm.

Nothing of what I had seen and done before was more painful for me, than to go with farmer Georges and his son, in their hay wagon pulled by their gray mare, to pick up the bodies of Michelle and the young man. We went across fields and, first, left the carriage at the farm with the young boy and his mother. We went carefully across the grove. The car had disappeared and the Germans with it. There was no immediate danger. Farmer Georges and his son went back to bring the carriage around the grove.

I was alone with Michelle. I felt as if all my blood had abandoned my veins. My shirt was still covering her face. I wished that I had been killed with her. We would have appeared together in front of God to ask His forgiveness for having made love without His permission and, perhaps, would He give us a late benediction. But then, the very precise sensations that were mine when making love with Michelle came back to my mind and, for an instant, I became madly furious. "It's of no use," I thought after calming down. "She is dead, and nothing will bring her back to me."

I slowly pulled my shirt. Her face looked rested, almost with a smile on her lips. I thought that she now resembled a statue of an angel in a cathedral, like statues certainly appeared during the Middle Age when they were delicately painted with the colors of life. Or was it my imagination? Michelle had not yet lost all traces of life but her lips, when I touched them, were already stiff. I put my shirt back on her face. I preferred to remember her as she still was.

At the pace of the gray mare pulling the hay wagon over the grass of the fields, we went slowly back to farmer Georges' place where I borrowed a bicycle to go immediately to the mission.

No one around had enough wood available to make two coffins, and trying to collect lumber would be a difficult task that would require much time and could be dangerous. We decided to bury Michelle and the young man wrapped in bed sheets.

All the members of Marc's group wanted to gather at night to bury her in the small village cemetery. I was not happy with the idea of everybody's meeting at night in the cemetery, but the boys could not be dissuaded, and I gave up. When they had word of it, the members of the mission did not believe that Michelle was dead. They believed it only when I came to tell them. They agreed not to go to the cemetery as a precaution. The life of the mission was more important than Michelle's life. Mine was expendable.

At one in the morning, the whole group gathered, invisible, around the cemetery, which fortunately was on the side of the hamlet. Georges and P'tit Louis alerted by Marc had already begun to dig with two other men. Only those four men were visible, but all the other men had a gun at hand. Georges, P'tit Louis, and the two other men had brought the two bodies to the cemetery and deposited them close to the holes. It took the four diggers almost an hour to dig two holes large and deep enough. Then, in a gesture of defiance, all the men came out openly and gathered around them. Father Durand appeared suddenly, surging from nowhere, with his stole around his neck. He shortened the prayer for the dead but said a few emotional words about Michelle. He knew her as a partner in the Resistance. Some of the tough guys were crying. I still believed that I was in the midst of a nightmare and was going to wake up. But I also knew that it was not true, and that they were really putting Michelle in her grave. As their leader, I had to show my men an example of courage in adversity. After Father Durand, I said a few words, taking on myself the challenge not to reveal my emotion. I also said a few words about an unknown young man. Then I ordered everyone to disperse, but they did not until the last one of them threw a handful of earth on Michelle's body. I remained with the four men until the graves were covered. Father Durand, who had also remained with us, had prepared two wooden crosses that he planted at the head of the two graves and recited a last prayer.

Then Georges said, "Guys, it's three in the morning. Let's go to my place. The patron will prepare something for us. Sorry to say so, but after that work, I am starving. Poor Michelle, that will not make her come back. What about you?" Father Durand, P'tit Louis, and I agreed that we were starving. "Let's go!' said Georges.

Bernadette was in the kitchen. She was waiting for her man to come back, eventually with some others. With her neighbor, she had taken care of Michelle's body to give her a decent appearance, even if no one was going to see her. She had dressed her in the clean clothes that Michelle's sponsors, tutors, parents, or whoever they were, a couple of farmers that Bernadette did not know, had brought. "She was not of our family," they finally said. "Her father is a farm machinery salesman. Michelle was our goddaughter. She went to school until eighteen and wanted to go on. We don't even know where her parents are actually. They left her with us before the invasion to go to Normandy to bring Michelle's grandmother, the mother of her mother, here. We told them that it was crazy but they went anyway. We have not heard from them since they left."

They were absolutely ravaged by Michelle' death. When her godmother, Germaine, saw her on the straw, in the barn, with her white face and her blouse red with blood, she fainted. "We put her, first, in the barn, with the young man" said Bernadette, "You never can tell. If the German had come to search the house, we could have thrown hay over them."

The stove was roaring and the eggs were waiting to become an omelet that became a vast omelet. The fresh goat cheese was put on the table with an open bottle of white wine, still warm boiled potatoes, and fresh onion. "Put your legs under the table," Bernadette said with authority. "And eat! Now I go to bed."

For several days, I remained in a very gloomy mood, profoundly affected by the absurdity of Michelle's death. I tried, apparently successfully, not to show my despair to Mary and I went to all my duties as usual. The fanatic Marika was eventually explainable. Germany was still all-powerful in France and the Gestapo active when she contacted me. They still had the time and means to work on counter terrorism. Not anymore. We were coming closer to the conclusion of our underground war. What remained in the south of France of the German army was in full retreat, but, yet, there were still some unpredictable packs of fanatics whose motivations were losing any significance. They were, nevertheless, able to kill up to the last minute, if they had an occasion to do so, like those who killed Michelle and the young man.

Germans were certainly fighting like devils in Normandy, but in our area, deprived of logistical support, certainly discouraged by endless and dangerous kilometers, the retreat was taking the shape of a rout for many of them. Two days before, while going to Prince by the back roads, I saw from afar, on a road crossing the one I was on, a movement of German vehicles. I stopped and did not even bother to camouflage the car. There was a house on the side of the road, almost at the crossing. I believe they did not pay any attention to me. I reached the house and remained in its shadow to have a close look at the commotion.

The best piece of retreating equipment that I saw, among others that were not in a better shape, was a "Viva Grand Sport" convertible Renault, a huge and beautiful car, a black body with red leather seats, carrying five officers. The Renault had been equipped with a wood burning gasogene that emerged five feet above the trunk into which it was fixed. The bottom of the burner was dark red. It proved that a great melting problem was under development. Even better, the car was running on the rim of its wheels, all tires missing.

I tried to imagine the thoughts going through the minds of those men who perhaps had participated in extraordinary pageants like those of Nuremberg with immaculate uniforms and scintillating boots. They had conquered Europe; now they looked miserable in that disfigured car. I was alone and could do nothing. It was of no use to try alerting one of our groups. They were too far away. But even if those men passed unscathed throughout our whole area, they were far from Germany. The five in the Renault would certainly be obliged to abandon their vehicle a few kilometers farther on and walk when the core of the burner would have finally melted down.

We had requisitioned for our own purpose all vehicles that could run. Those that the Germans could eventually discover in some barns were cars that were too old or had not run since the beginning of the war. They were unable to put them on the road. Many of the cars that we utilized were mostly in the same state when we found them, but we had mechanics, who could spend hours on an engine. And we had gas while the lack of gas was a plague affecting the German retreat.

It was such a plague that, a few days later, having exceptionally passed the night at my grandmother's house, and crossing the piazza to pick up my car that was hidden in the barn of Marc's farm, I saw a young man on a bicycle, pedaling in my direction. He called me, and I waited for him.

"There are eighteen thousand Germans with a lot of trucks and big guns stopped ten kilometers from here," he said.

"What do you mean by big guns?"

"Big guns on wheels."

"How do you know they are eighteen thousand?"

"Because they said so."

"And why did they stop?"

"They say that some of their trucks are out of gas. They cannot go any farther, and they want to surrender, but they don't want to surrender to the resistance."

"Why?"

"Because they say that the resistance would kill them. They want an Allied officer."

"And why did they send you?"

"Because I was the only one with a bicycle, and the only one who knew where I could find someone like you."

"And how do you know that?"

"I was not coming to see you. I was going to my grandaunt's farm. Marc's mother is my aunt. I know that Marc is involved in the resistance, and I hoped to find him... or you. I saw your car several times in the barn."

So much for the secret! It did not matter anymore. Gestapo or reprisals were out, but the whole area was more or less aware of what we were doing.

"OK!" I said. "Go back and tell the Germans that, in two hours from now, an officer of the British Army will come to discuss their surrender."

I rushed to Mary and drove her and Peter full speed to the huge German convoy stopped in the middle of flat fields so that the resistance could not surprise them. The "commandant's" plane had spotted the convoy early in the morning. The pilot could not figure out why they had not tried to shoot him down. He declared that he made a second pass very low but that they had not reacted. Nothing!

"Strange!" the "commandant" said. "We will find out." But neither he nor Prince commented about the plane's flight. Prince and the "commandant" were already readying for action, but they were far away from the convoy, and eighteen thousand men with big guns, were a huge morsel to swallow. In any case, it was impossible to attack them where they were. In a fast move, if it were possible, the "commandant" and Prince would join Marc who was in a better position to act. They agreed that the best they could do without losing too many men would be to slow them.

I had already seen at very close range a huge German convoy, not so huge as this one, but one with tanks and incendiary grenades. This one had no tanks but "guns on wheels" as the young boy put it. As soon as Mary introduced herself, the commanding German officer, who spoke English relatively well, gave Mary and Peter an impeccable salute. The long column was in perfect order, all soldiers sitting in their trucks. After a few minutes of exchanges between Mary and the officer, Mary asked me to rush to Prince and the "commandant" to give them an explanation of the situation. They had orders not to move, but to provide the Germans with gas. I also had to go and tell Marc to stay put and do nothing.

"That's the best of the best," Prince laughed when I told him about the gas. "They are going to ruin me! We will go with their own trucks to give them some of their own gas with the original octane. They will love it when they see the delivery trucks! I don't have oil to mix with the gas, except for our own cars. That's the only revenge we can take, but they will reach the Allied lines."

"Well," the "commandant" said, "Maybe it's better like that. I am sure that we would have lost some men to get the same result. In any case, this is the proof that we, and all the other guys that we don't know, did a good job. They don't want to surrender to us."

There were effectively eighteen thousand men. They said that they were coming from garrisons at the Spanish border, but that they had practically exhausted all the gas they carried and had suffered violent attacks by the resistance, which is why they did not want to surrender to the resistance. I suppose that Mary gave them a realistic rendering of their situation. They had no chance to go any farther than the 200 kilometers' worth of gas that we were giving them. They would find nothing to eat for eighteen thousand men. They had no other solution than to go north to surrender to the Allied forces with our benediction and a nice piece of paper signed by Mary.

They were lucky. The war was over for them. The threat that had been made via German flyers, to transform the "terrorists" into meat for pâté, acted like a boomerang. They feared a reciprocal action by the resistance, but the threat was an abstraction. I don't know how we could have transformed them into meat for sausages. We certainly did not have the means or the will to do it. But they seemed to be so traumatized by their encounters with the resistance that Mary's strong words were seemingly enough to take any stupid idea out of their minds. They accepted Mary's conditions. Mary was taking a risk but it was a calculated risk, and it worked out very well.

I left Mary and Peter talking with the German officer to go to Prince and the "commandant" and, afterward, to go tell Marc that he didn't need to do anything, only to stay "home" with his men.

What followed was a big parade of German trucks, many trucks pulling a gun, in the streets of the villages they had to pass through. It was a big parade with no music and no cheers. No other noises than those of truck engines and tires on the pavement were perceptible. The trucks were in good condition and had decent tires. They did not resemble those units that had lost their material, and were pillaging what they could find to get out of a desperate situation. At the windows, in the doors, in the streets people were silent. I know it because I was at a friendly window watching the long cortège of trucks full of soldiers who were not waving at the population. In fact, they were also singularly silent. After their passage, the comments went on.

"It's over," I thought. I put my hand in the small pocket on the left side of my shirt. The little capsule was still there. It had followed me from one shirt to the next. I took it delicately and, bending, put it on the ground in front of me. I put my right shoe on top of it and, slowly, smashed it.

Only a few sporadic events took place during the following days. One of them gave me an occasion to beat the "commandant" at his own game. The "commandant" had always managed to get one up on us with his cars like the Dodge or the small convertible Renault that he was driving once in a while. He had some others. He never told me where he found them. All our cars were notably less classy than his. It was also true that he was the only person with a plane in his inventory of armaments. He was wearing some kind of a fantasy uniform made to order by a good tailor that he was the only one to know. When he stepped down from the convertible, you could believe that he was coming straight from the racetrack, the golf club, or a cocktail at the casino.

However, driving to Prince's and arriving in front of the farmhouse, I had to beep the horn. The "commandant" had not seen me coming, and I did not want to lose the pleasure of my showing off. When he saw me, he almost fainted. "Where did you find that?" was his first question.

He turned around, and around. "What in exchange?" he asked.

"It's not for sale."

"Come on! You would not do that to me?"

"Don't try to take me by my sentiments, please. OK! OK! What do you give in exchange?"

"The Dodge and the Renault."

"Two for one! You will regret it."

"The Dodge, then!"

That is how the "commandant" came to sit at the wheel of a brand-new Packard convertible, white from head to tail and as red inside as a cooked lobster, a beautiful machine. The commandant let his hands go all around, caressing the wheel, the dashboard, and the seats. On the back seat was a wooden suitcase. When he saw it, he asked me what it was.

"It's part of the deal," I answered. "It's a surprise for you that comes with the car. I suggest that you don't grab it by the handle. I did, and that's why I suggest that you not do it if you don't want to risk a heart attack."

I almost had the heart attack when I grabbed the wooden suitcase by its handle to take it out of the car and see what was inside. I had stepped on the rear seat to pull it up and deposit it on the ground without opening the passenger door. I must say that it was heavy, but that was not enough to discourage a young man in his twenties. The suitcase was out of the car, already on its side and ready to be deposited on the ground when it opened. A noise of objects falling in disorder on each other with a metallic sound required my immediate attention. I looked down at the ground, and on the ground was a messy pile of little round German hand grenades.

I did not even think at jumping on the other side of the car to be more or less protected by its body if one of those burst, blowing up the whole damned thing. I remained immobile, petrified, stupid, standing on the back seat of the car, and expecting I did not know what. Perhaps I was expecting my death? After a reasonable number of seconds, I breathed. I could have left those grenades where they were, but I thought that someone or some children could find them, manipulate them, and explode them. So I decided to put them back in the wooden suitcase. I did not count them. I was not in the mood for that.

"That does not tell me where you got that car."

"That's another story," I answered.

I had been told by one of our people that a small unit of Germans, in the evening, with two trucks, a small bus, and a white car had invaded the castle that was previously my "National Museum," forced the gate, and were camping behind. From what was known, they had not tried to go into the castle. Supposedly in charge of the castle's security, I went immediately to Prince and asked him to lend me a German prisoner, and have his translator explain to him that he was now an emissary of the French Resistance. The prisoner, a man of no significance in his forties, small and baldheaded, did not seem to appreciate his honorary role. He had to carry a message to the troops occupying the castle. They had to surrender or leave at the first light of dawn if they did not wish to be massacred by the resistance. I am sure that my prisoner would have preferred to stay in the woods, away from the vicissitudes of war. But he had no alternative. For once I took a gun that I ostentatiously put in my belt in front of my delegate.

I took my man as close to the gate as I could without risking being massacred by the German campers instead of them by us. He knew what he had to do, and crossed the space in front of the gate with a piece of white cloth that he agitated above his head. His compatriots opened the gate for him and closed it. One of those men, perhaps an officer shouted something. I did not understand what it was because, as you know, I don't speak German. Maybe it was only one word, "Nuts?" My prisoner had definitively lost his freedom.

I turned around the wall of the castle, jumped over it, and knocked at the usual window. My friends had anxiously watched the invasion but had also ascertained that the Germans were camping just behind the gate with no apparent intention to move deeper in the park. I told them about the ultimatum. They had seen the German with his white flag going in. It was my sole action as "protector" of the castle and of the precious treasures of Le Louvre.

I remained in the castle. All I know is that it was still dark when they left in the morning, certainly after a lousy night, like ours, leaving behind them a small bus and the white car. We never figured out why they abandoned them. They certainly required too much gas, especially the white car that was not of much use for them. I could not figure out where they had found the white car. It was recent and did not show even one scratch.

"Now, commandant," I added. "The grenades are yours. I suppose that you can use them, and also the small bus. It is part of the deal. You have to pick it up. We cannot leave it where it is. But, please, recognize that I beat you with my car."

"You rested your case! Let's drink to it!"

We did. Prince joined. The Dodge was too big for me and less maneuverable than my Citroën. I gave it to Marc.

All of us had the feeling that it was over. Germans were no longer sighted on our roads. I took advantage of that fact to organize the collection of milk that had been discontinued for months. We had trucks driven by our men that were now visiting the farms in the morning. Milk was a good complement for the diet of our forest dwellers. Everybody was happy especially the farmers who were able to make some money out of their milk, but it became evident after a few days that we did not have enough stomachs to absorb the whole production of the local cows and goats.

I paid a visit to a *fromagerie,* or cheese producer if you prefer, and asked the owner to go back to production with the milk that we would deliver at his door. Everybody seemed to be happy to see that life was finally coming back after a long nightmare.

The liberation of Paris was officially announced on August 24, 1944. We made it the official day of our own liberation. We knew perfectly well that the war with Germany was far from being over, but a great wind of symbolic freedom and joy blew over us. It was, of course, an occasion for immediate celebration.

We celebrated.

The following morning, I was advised that I had to take care of a very serious situation that was causing much consternation all around. I went straight to Mary.

"We have a problem with the so-called Colonel Charles and his communist group," I told her, "and we need your help."

"Who is 'we'?" Mary asked.

"The others and myself. I know! Don't tell me! But I am still French first, anyway. Listen! Charles and his men have occupied the seat of the local government, the prefecture, the post offices, the regional newspaper, and they block the roads. Everyone has to ask and wait for a pass to travel. They have established controls on the roads. Don't forget that they have enough people to do that, all the people for whom Charles asked for the weapons that we refused to give him, thank God! They all can be transformed into bureaucrats delivering passes to travel or publishing a communist newspaper. I know that it is none of our business, but we cannot let Charles occupy the area in the name of communism. We had the German controls, and now we have the communist controls. All our men are ready to go against them. After the failure of Jean, our so called "new commandant", and in the absence of any other military authority in our area, you must use your moral authority. Coming from you, if you say 'go,' they will go."

"You were right about the communists," Mary answered me. "They were waging their own war. They wanted to take over the country at the liberation. They believe that they are making the red revolution and will transform France into a communist country. I am not supposed to ask you that question, but what do you want me to do in that mess? What do you expect from me?"

"An order for mobilizing Prince's, the "commandant's," and Marc's forces. It's more than two thousand men. Prince is waiting for that order. He cannot stand Charles. The 'commandant' never forgot that they blew the bridge in front of 'his' plane. Personally, I cannot forget either that they put their guns in my back. We will ask Prince to bring an ultimatum to Charles. I am sure that Prince will be delighted to deliver it himself. The ultimatum will be very simple: You get lost or we disarm you, by force if necessary. If you give the order, you unify the noncommunist Resistance. They know that they depended on you for their fight against the Germans, and your moral caution is enough for them."

"OK!" Mary answered. "Go! You have your orders, but the ultimatum comes from the concerted chiefs of the resistance, not from us. Do as you say, but you, personally, are not involved. And that, also, is an order! Sorry, but you are still a member of the mission and the mission cannot intervene in French affairs."

Prince, the "commandant," and Marc had enough vehicles to put several hundred men with considerable armament on the road. That was again an operation without my participation. As foreseen, Prince took a great pleasure, tinted with vengeance, at delivering the ultimatum to Charles personally, forcing his roadblocks with trucks overflowing with men "armed to their teeth."

A few hours later, all roadblocks disappeared. The red revolution was out of order. Charles had tried, but with a lot of illusions about his capability to succeed, even locally. If the communists wanted France to become communist, it was not to be at the barrel of a gun. They had to use other ways.

The unified intervention of Prince, the "commandant," and Marc re-established the threatened democracy in their sector. The British mission witnessed the fact, as it was its only role.

"It will be your last mission," Mary told me the next day. I want you to go to Paris tomorrow, to the Ministry of War, to deliver an envelope to the person whose name will appear on the envelope. No receipt, just delivery, but it has to be done by hands that I can trust."

"I appreciate the compliment."

"Shut up, you stupid!" Mary said, losing her British composure in front of me for the first time since I had met her. I had a sincere admiration for her. She had always seemed to be perfectly in control of herself in any circumstance. She had been more than efficient in her job. If the underground groups had succeeded in her area as they did, she had a large part of responsibility for that success.

"You know that I will do that for you with pleasure."

"Don't become sentimental. The "commandant" will provide you with a different car from your eternal Citroën. I trust you, but I don't trust your Citroën. The car will be here tonight. Leave early tomorrow. As long as you will be in Paris, I give you three days of freedom. You are aware that we are still at war, still in the army, and I don't want to give you more. Never can tell, even now!"

"I appreciate that, again. I suppose that my parents are in Paris. In any case, I will be happy to see Paris again. What kind of a car?"

The car sent by the "commandant" arrived in the afternoon. I had already seen American cars but none labeled Lincoln Zephyr. It was certainly one of the latest imported models from before the war. It looked as if it was just out of the showroom of a car dealer. By French standards, it was an oversized American car, twelve cylinders, two doors, fishtail, "metallic" green (as green as it was possible to be green), and with large white stripes on the tires. "I don't need so many cylinders," I thought. "Half of them would have been enough!" With its pointed hood, it resembled a boat more than a light breeze. Or perhaps that car could float over the road like a breeze. I would find out the next day.

Only the "commandant" was able to provide such a car. Where had he found it? I was sure that he was sending it to me to top me again after the "Packard" episode. He was sorry to be unable to deliver it himself and pay us a visit. He hoped, nonetheless, that the car would be adequate for a trip to the capital. Mary was also giving me access to an American gas depot, which already existed on the way to Paris. I could refuel for the security of the gas gauge, aside from the ten gallons of gas that I would carry in its trunk.

I wondered how Mary could already know that there was gas on the way to Paris. I realized once more that I was not in the "secrets of the gods" but abstained from questioning her, according to the rule of no-questions-asked. I also realized that, among other things, I had never been informed of the content of the radio exchanges between the mission and London. I did not even know, most of the time, where the radio was operating from, or what Henry, the fourth member of the mission and direct assistant to Mary, was doing. Every one of us was acting in a personal sphere, ignoring the others' activities. Only Mary knew and coordinated our actions.

The rumor flew fast that a car was going to Paris the next day. In one hour there were more applications than the car could carry, all from men. I accepted five passengers with no other luggage than their toothbrushes. At six in the morning, we hit the road, three on the front seat and three on the back seat. A button changed the speedometer from miles to kilometers. With a sharp angle, the shift handle passed through the dashboard to be located almost at the level of the wheel for the ease of the driver. According to my judgment, the car was a mixture of power and indolence, if that word could describe a car. It was almost new and it ran perfectly well until we reached the American depot. The car was superb to look at, but its gas consumption was also superb.

"I don't know why I am driving that flying cloud," I thought. "I would have done as well with my Citroën. With the Citroën, you don't need to turn the wheel three times before the car begins turning, but the seating is not as comfortable. With this one, you seem to be relaxing on your home sofa. I like very much the "commandant" but, once in a while, he is a little show off. I don't know whom he wanted to impress with this car. Never mind, let's get some gas here."

It was not really a depot, only piles of gas cans and two trucks that looked as if they had been abandoned on the side of the road. Two soldiers came alongside the car when I stopped. They were the first Americans that any of the car's passengers had ever seen. One minute later, they were almost kissing the uniformed guys. I presented my order of requisition, and a full jerrycan of gas was poured into the gas tank. Time to thank the commanding sergeant who had allotted the gas, say goodbye, and we were on the road

207

again. I was driving at a decent speed. Any speed was decent because there was no other vehicle in sight, but, all of a sudden, the engine coughed several times, died abruptly, and refused to start again.

So much for a car more dependable than my Citroën! I will say a thing or two about it to Mary and the "commandant" when I get back. "Is there a mechanic on board?" I asked. I did not believe my ears when one of the passengers answered yes. "But," added the passenger, "I don't know this type of car. If it is a very classic breakdown, it will be OK. Otherwise, we are in trouble."

Everyone got out of the car. All the passengers and I took advantage of the situation to satisfy our bladders' needs, after which the mechanic disappeared into the engine. "Do we have tools?" he asked. I knew that there was a bundle of new tools in the trunk in a bag marked Lincoln. After ten minutes, the mechanic exited from under the hood to say, "Those bastards, you know what they gave us with their gas? Guess! Water! There was water in their gas. They surely sell part of the gas and replace it with water. We almost kissed them, and this is what they gave us in exchange! Perhaps those who gave us the gas didn't even know it and were not responsible. Come on, nice people! We would do the same thing to buy a drink."

Comments by the others were devoid of amenity, but the mechanic was already at the back of the car. "The water is at the bottom of the tank," he said. "One bolt and I clean it. I hope we don't have too much of it. I will clean the gas line and we can go. If you come back the same way, you can stop to thank those guys."

I will not say anything to Mary and the "commandant" when I get back about the dependability of the Lincoln – only about the dependability of American gas.

Farther on, the car was stopped again, this time by a huge soldier with a sign on his helmet and armband reading "MP." No one, including me, had any idea of what MP meant. The man came to the window to say, almost apologetically, that he was sorry but there was no bridge left across the Loire. We had to make a one-hundred-kilometers detour to cross the river on a canal bridge. The sides were wide enough for cars to pass by.

One hundred kilometers later, I faced the canal bridge. The metal bridge crossed the river carrying the canal in its heavy U shape. The paths on both sides of the bridge offered just enough room for cars. I drove very slowly. The Zephyr was broad and the path comparatively narrow. I was so attentive that I did not notice a group of twenty or twenty-five soldiers, all with red caps, waiting for us at the end of the bridge. All of them, thumbs up, were apparently desirous to get on board to go to Paris. I did not stop and went slowly through the group that opened in front of me, the red cap men understanding, but with disappointment, that the car was already full.

When we reached Paris at Porte d'Orléans, the Zephyr became a taxi. No public transportation of any kind was available. Except for military vehicles, the boulevards and streets were empty. With my passengers living at the four corners of Paris, it took me more than two hours to deliver the five men to their destinations. Finally, I was able to drive back to the center of town. My parents' apartment was located on Rue Caumartin, a short street opening on the Grands Boulevards and close to the Opéra. I stopped the car at number twenty-five, in front of a large double door closing the entrance of a theatre, the Comédie Caumartin. The apartment was in the building topping the theatre.

Then, the incredible happened. Anything can happen, including the most incredible. I had not stopped the

Zephyr's engine when I heard a screech in the back of my car. Glancing at the rear mirror, I saw a car, a big black Peugeot looking like the last prewar model. A man opened the driver's door, literally jumped in the street, and rushed to my open window. The uniformed man was wearing a red beret.

We looked at each other in silence for a fraction of second before the man with the red beret said quietly, purposely quietly, and with a pretense of detachment, "When your brother, on the canal bridge, puts his thumb up to go to Paris, can't you take him on board?" And, in the middle of the street, we fell in each other arms with shouts of joy. After two years of separation, absolutely ignorant of each other's fate, we had arrived, exactly at the same minute, at the entrance to our parents' apartment. "Nobody will ever believe it, not even our parents," I commented.

Several windows opened, and a door also opened on the side of the theatre's portal. That door allowed the people living in the building to go in and out without being obliged to open the large portal. The "concierge" came out and looked at the two of us. The only thing that she was able to say was, "Oh, monsieur Michel! Oh, monsieur Christian!" and she started crying aloud. When she was again able to talk, it was to tell us that our parents had left that very same morning in a military car in the direction of La Baule. We had just missed them by a few hours, but we were happy to learn that they were alive and apparently in good shape.

"I did not recognize you at first sight, I recognized the car," Christian said. "Where did you pick up that green machine? Who has ever seen such a green color?"

"Then, how come, if you were hitching a ride on the bridge, that you are here, driving that battered Peugeot?"

"Don't bother! Let's celebrate!" Christian shouted. "We should put the green car into the porch of the theatre, close the door, and use the Peugeot. We will be less visible. Nobody drives such a green thing in France today! The theatre has not been active for three years. I asked the concierge. It's perfect!"

"I am on an official mission," I said. "I must go to the Ministry of War at once, Place de la Concorde, to deliver a message. It's not far away. Come with me. We walk. After that, I have three free days in front of me."

"I have four days myself! Let's go!"

While walking slowly to the Ministry of War, I told Christian my story and, while walking slowly back to Rue Caumartin, he told me his.

Christian explained to me how, from one bus to another, he reached the Spanish border close to Prats de Mollo, the last village on a road that ended there. During the night, he passed the border to find himself at la Gardia Civile for breakfast. Without any identification papers, he declared that he was Canadian, afraid to be sent back to France if he declared that he was French.

He sojourned three months in a jail where life was difficult. The cells were so crowded that they had to take turns to sleep on the floor. The food was of the same quality as the comfort and very parsimonious, even for the jailers who were no better served than their prisoners. With a lot of money, it was possible to get some food from outside. The only rich man in their cell, and Christian mentioned that he never asked him how he had been able to keep his treasure, was a Jewish jeweler who ordered some fried eggs when it was possible. On receipt of the eggs, he divided them equally among his cell's companions.

The only accessible distraction was the Sunday mass. Everyone attended it, even if with no other motivation than being able to walk a few steps. Christian said that the most depressing moment was hearing once in a while in the morning a firing squad passing by to execute some Republicans in the courtyard of the prison. The civil war had ended long ago but executions were still going on.

After three months, he was transferred to a camp named Miranda. Compared to his first jail, Miranda, despite its bad reputation, was practically, he said, a one-star hotel. He spent six months in Miranda, wondering every day what the next day would bring, and if he would ever be able to get out of Spain and join the French forces in North Africa.

After those six months, and to his utmost surprise, he was liberated and put in charge of an official representative of the Canadian government. "Happy to get you out of here," said the representative, "but you are an expensive man, and only a supposed Canadian. We, nevertheless, exchanged you for a bag of corn. That was your price."

With a small group of other men, he was put aboard a train to Lisbon where the Portuguese Red Cross welcomed them with an enormous pile of cans of sardines. After an indigestion of sardines, which were served without bread or seasoning, as none had been available for a long time, they were transported to the harbor where they boarded a French frigate. The sailors were more than happy to rescue some men who had visibly suffered in Spanish camps and jails. They did not know what to do to please them. "What can we do for you that you would like?" they asked. After months with only water, the unanimous answer was wine.

They disembarked in Algiers where Christian was immediately incorporated into the French army, the Giraud Army. One month later, completely disenchanted by the politically oriented spirit of that army, he deserted to embark clandestinely on a boat sailing for England. He kept hidden until the boat was on the high seas. From the moment he came out of hiding, he kept company for the rest of the voyage with a bunch of pigs occupying the cell next to his in the belly of the ship. Sailing for England from North Africa, the boat crossed the Atlantic to join a convoy close to the Canadian shores. It was a long trip. By the time they reached England days later, without having been torpedoed, the pigs and he had finally become friends.

It was camp life again in England, this time with decent food and accommodations. The tough part of the day was the interrogation conducted every morning by courteous military officers. "Where were you living in Paris? Can you describe your street and its endings? You were a student at the Lycée Condorcet. Can you describe the Lycée and your classroom? Who were your teachers? Can you describe them? Where were you or your parents shopping? Can you describe the stores? What was your closest subway station?" Precise questions followed precise questions.

According to the answers, a different interrogator was taking charge. Some of the answers were directly verified in France. That was what one of the officers told him at the end of his interrogation. The interrogation lasted for a whole month and during that month two German spies were detected. They had lived in France, but certainly not long enough to acquire all the necessary details. The final question was to ask him in what unit he would like to serve. Paratrooper was his answer.

The paratroopers survived in England despite the nights of leave that ended up many times in brawls and fights with the police. The Britons, hard-boiled eggs, if there ever were any, were always ready for a fight. During or after the fight, the main problem was to escape arrest by the police because you would reappear at your unit the next morning with one or two black eyes that substituted for reports that the cops did not want to fill.

After months and months of patience, they finally opened their chutes in the sky of Normandy during the night of the fifth to the sixth of June, 25 kilometers off Sainte Mère l'Eglise to create a diversion confusing the Germans.

"They told us that Russian troops were among the German troops, and that we had everything to fear from them. In fact, it was true. We learned later that a group of paratroopers unfortunately landed in a Russian encampment. They were all killed, but the Russians were so surprised that they started shooting at random without even looking at whom they were shooting and they killed a good number of their own. They were ex-prisoners of the Germans. They had volunteered to join the Vlassov army, which had been incorporated into the German army. They were famous for their atrocities

"We regrouped easily in the middle of the night. We had to wait until dawn to move. We were of course completely silent when we heard noises. We reinforced our defensive position and waited, eyes wide open, ready for the worst, I mean the Russians. Nothing happened. We moved as soon as the first glimmer of dawn allowed us to see enough to know where we were going. So far, we had not been attacked. We discovered that the Russians were, in reality, a few cows completely indifferent to what was going on around them.

"That was our first encounter with the enemy. One of our men asked if we were taking prisoners or shooting them. That was the last joke. There were plenty of Germans around. They started to move like us when daylight came back, and a few minutes later, it was hell. At one point, when reaching a farm, our avant-garde was received by machine guns firing, invisibly, from behind a hedgerow. I was part of the avant-garde... We were six. I was one of the two survivors. Now, not a quarter of my unit is still alive. I have been lucky. I went through the whole campaign, so far, without a scratch. Why him and not me? Only God knows.

"Our mission was to disrupt the German means of transportation by commando operations in front of advancing Allied forces. We even learned how to drive locomotives, and also their weak points to learn how to insert a small magnetic explosive device to disable them. We had to slow down the German reinforcements as much as we could. We both succeeded and failed many times. I must say that the Resistance and the railroad people did not hesitate to risk their lives to help us. But we were soon absorbed by the advancing Allied forces and reintegrated into them. You get it all!"

The following night, my brother and I agreed again that the nightclub was boring. It was time to go someplace else, a petit bistrot type if there were still one open for a last drink, or go back to Rue Caumartin. It was one in the morning when we were again in the street, leaving behind us the noise of the packed nightclub.

"Am I drunk?" Christian asked. "I see two of them."

"I have not drunk enough to be drunk," I said, "and I see two of them."

Two similar Peugeots, one almost touching the back of the other, were parked on the other side of the street. One was black and battered as if it had gone through a war; the other was black, shining, as beautiful as a groomed luxury dog.

"Such a car," Christian said, "can belong only to a B.O.F. (Beurre. Oeuf. Fromage: {butter, egg, cheese}). It's a black market or a mafia's car. I drive."

The owner of the car had not secured the doors. That was a mistake. Those cars had no ignition keys but a knob to pull to start the engine. Christian pulled the "starter" but nothing happened. Absolutely nothing.

"The son-of-a-bitch!" Christian said, "Give me a hand."

Christian who already knew the Peugeot from using "ours," opened the hood. "That's why," he said, showing the distributor. "He has the cap in his pocket, sure that nobody will deprive him of his wonder car. Let's make it snappy! He can come out at any moment."

Christian went back to "our" car, opened the hood, took off the cap, went to the other car, and replaced the missing cap. We jumped into the car that started right away and we left, leaving the hood of the other car open.

"I wish I could see his face when he comes out," Christian said. "He cannot complain too much. He still has a car! He saw our car when he parked on its back, but he never thought that what is now happening to him was possible. He should have used his door keys. He'll do it next time."

"You have some strange principles," I said after a silence.

"I have no principles," Christian answered "but a two-day leave for bringing a car to my unit. That's war! I went around a little yesterday while you were still sleeping. I negotiated a Jeep with an American. Very cheap! He needs the money. My unit will pay. He will say that someone stole it. I will paint over the white star. I have one day more than you have to stay in Paris. Today, I am going to give this one a beautiful army shade. I know where to get the paint. When you have gone, I will put the Jeep in the theatre and repaint it. The concierge will never talk and nobody passes in the theatre's hall. Day after tomorrow, I will go back to my base and come back to pick it up with another "para." Aside from the money, I have to negotiate the Jeep with my colonel."

"So, how much is a Jeep?" I asked.

"I don't know, but a Jeep is much more valuable than a trivial Peugeot. We are the poor parent in the Allied forces. They never give us enough Jeeps. One thing, now! We should go directly back to Rue Caumartin. Who knows if that man does not have an army behind him to search Paris tonight for his car?"

I was discovering a slightly different brother from the one I had put on a bus at La Sainte Beaume. The war had changed him, and I was wondering if it was for the best. My antiwar sentiments were growing inside of me, stronger than ever. Michelle's image came to my mind, and, all of a sudden, I talked again about her. My brother listened without a word.

"I know that your story is very dramatic," Christian finally said when I stopped talking. "But you can do nothing about it. It's the past. What happened was not your fault, and don't go for a guilt trip. If she had not died the way she did, are you sure that you loved her enough to put her really in your life? I mean to marry her. If you still want to be an artist, you'd better remain a bachelor for as long as you can. You will always find some girls to make love to. I learned one thing in England: when you see a girl that pleases you, put your hand on her ass. Two things: she slaps you on the face, but so what? Or she does not move. It's as simple as that. Here we are. Let's open the door without awakening the whole building. I have a pack of American cigarettes that I will give to the concierge tomorrow."

I did not ask my brother where the cigarettes were coming from. "This explains that," I thought, thinking about water in a gas can.

We kissed each other goodbye, displaying no more emotion than fitted two hardened warriors. The Peugeot was looking ugly under a coat of gray-green disgusting color. My brother had not painted the Lincoln, thank God! Now that he had transformed himself into a businessman in war supplies, I wondered if he would try to bribe me for an exchange. He did not. I always forgot, after the war, to ask him what he got from his colonel for the Jeep.

I had to go back to the mission. I wanted to stop at the gas depot on the road to say a few thank you words to the guy who provided me with first-rate gas, but I did not see the depot. I did not see it, or it had moved.

"I accomplished my mission," I told Mary. "I delivered it to proper hands."

"Thank you for that, but since you left I received orders from London. We are no longer operating as a British Mission. We have been ordered to go back to London. So, here is my question: do you want to come to London with me? You are officially an officer in the British army and part of our network. You could be useful. By the way, we are the only ones who provided a record of the money we received from London. We have special congratulations of our boss. I have to congratulate you personally as you were in charge of it. So, what do you want to do?"

"I would go with you with pleasure, but I am not British, and I speak a deplorable English. There is a French army. Forgive me, but I will join the French."

"I understand," Mary said. "Then, this is where we momentarily part. I am sure that we will meet again when I go to Paris. Here is an address where you will be able to get in touch with me. Leave your address at that address. Now, listen. I have two Legions of Honor to award. You said once that for being "always the only one" you deserved it. If you still want it, it's yours. I just have to put your name on a form, write down why you deserve it, and sign."

I did not even take the time to think. "You know how much I hate war. I want to be an artist, and I don't need to be reminded of my military exploits. In fact there were no exploits. I want to forget them completely. That rosette would permanently remind me of that damned war. I still cannot believe that Michelle died. I keep questioning myself about her death. If I had been more prudent, maybe nothing would have happened. My brother told me not to take a guilt trip about it, but I still feel bad when I think of her. And I also feel bad when I think of that young man and his mother, or of the two old people, and some others. I saved you, the men, myself, and others by killing Marika. She was responsible for her own death, but there is nothing more disgusting than taking a human life, I mean personally, in cold blood, not in the heat of battle. And you want to give me the Legion of Honor? You will find some guys who deserve it more than I do. If I had been wiser and had moved the camp the day before, as I vaguely wanted to, the first battle would have never taken place and the dead would be alive. You are very kind, but no thanks!"

"I understand," Mary said. I felt compassion in her voice. "But I agree with your brother: don't take a guilt trip about anything, or about Michelle. It's war, and wars call for casualties. You did very well; maybe better that some people more qualified than you would have done. You had a lot of responsibilities and were too young to have enough experience.... I myself made several mistakes. We did our best. I am going to tell you something about Michelle. I don't know if it will do you some good or not.... She really loved you. I know, I know because she gave me her confidence. She was afraid she was not good enough for you, but she loved you. I don't know if you ever loved her, I mean really, beside the emotion created by her death in your arms."

Apparently, Michelle had not told Mary that we had made love, or, maybe, she did not have the time to tell her.

"She was a nice and pure girl," Mary was saying, "Had she lived, you might have destroyed her. She didn't say a word, but she was sick to death during the few days she thought that you had another girl in your life, the so-called

Marika. It is how I discovered that she loved you. She knew of Marika through your friend Marc. I must say that Marc ignored her love for you. She came back to life when she learned that the other girl was out. She would have given her life for you." Mary stopped talking and her face took on a strange expression. "Maybe she did," she said after a silence that I did not want to break. "Maybe that's exactly what she did. According to what you told me, she was running behind you. Why was she running behind you instead of in front of you? Because she started to run a fraction of second after you did. You were running. Running under fire is no time for courtesy, and usually men run faster than women." Mary made a short pause. "She followed you, and she took the bullets that would have killed you."

"She did not even know my real name!"

Mary smiled.

"It does not matter. That she called you René or Michel would have changed nothing. No more than it would have changed something for you to learn that her real name was Michelle. You will always think of her with more affection than if I had not told you what just came through my mind. You owe her your life, but keep it as your secret. You have your whole life in front of you.. It is well known that time erases many things and many pains. As you said, you don't need the Legion of Honor. It would not help you. Let me kiss you goodbye. I never kissed you, but you deserve it."

She kissed me on both cheeks.

"This has more value for me than the Legion of Honor," I said, trying to keep up at the level of the circumstance.

Mary looked at me with her light blue eyes. "Do you always talk to women like that?"

"I try, but this is exceptional."

"Get out of here!"

That was the last time I spoke with her before her departure for England.

One week later, I received a message. The commanding officer of the "castle affair," a colonel, was in jail. Without gas, his unit had never been able to go further than a few miles. I could visit him if I wished, and there I was. He had been momentarily put in a municipal jail and not sent to a prisoners' camp. When interrogated, he revealed that he was involved in several operations of the "castle" type and was set apart as a possible war criminal.

The colonel was wearing his German uniform and saluted me when I came in. We were in a small room that was equally parted by a low wall and vertical bars running from the wall to the ceiling. It resembled a parlor of a nuns' convent, but I was not going to talk with a nun. I had several questions in mind and was not at all interested in the story of his life. The colonel was speaking a broken but understandable French.

I feared the answer to my first question. I was, perhaps, going to learn if some of my men had been made prisoners. To my utmost despair that I did not show in front of him, he answered that they found four men trying to hide in the dependencies. For whatever reason, they had not managed to fly away.

"We did not kill them," he said. "They had to be taken alive." The whole operation was under the command of the Gestapo. He was only a hand executing his orders. He had never been a Nazi. He was giving as proof of it the fact that he had formerly forbidden any destruction during each one of his operations.

"What about the two farmers that your men killed?"

"Which farmers? I never heard of that. Had I, I would have arrested and punished my men. I am a decent officer."

He went on to say that his father also was an officer in the German army during World War One. Personally, he loved music and poetry, and music and poetry do not get along with destruction and murder. He insisted on the fact that he was not responsible for what had happened. The Gestapo was.

"What about your men in the sidecar?" I asked. "Why didn't you retaliate by burning the "castle"?

"The Gestapo was already gone. As soon as they arrested your men and the two old people who were living in the house, they went. I had no reason for burning the buildings. You would be here today accusing me for that. I am innocent. I took no lives. The Gestapo did. And I destroyed no property."

I could not figure out if the colonel was telling me the truth about himself or testing on me his future defense based on the excuse that he was strictly performing orders that he had to fulfill. Was he sincere with his affirmation that he was not a Nazi but a decent old-fashioned officer? Or had he been clever enough, foreseeing, at least in France, the defeat of the German armies and his eventual capture, to act as if he were a decent old-fashioned officer?

When I told him about the armored convoy, their exactions, and the burning of houses, he only mentioned the fact that those were "real Nazis." And when I asked him what had become of my four men and the two old people, he answered that he did not know. "Gestapo," he insisted again.

The "castle affair" had cost only eight lives. It meant that we had been lucky because he had not enough men to surround the woods. Thus, a military operation had become a vulgar police operation; otherwise we would all have been trapped. At that moment, I hated that man, but I had a question to ask: how did they know about our existence, where we were, and how many we were?

I had always thought that we had been betrayed by a spy. My conclusion was correct. Among all the young people that we accepted was a spy. The colonel had never known his name and whereabouts. Of course! Thus, it banned any possibility of following the trail. I would have followed that trail to the end of the world to put the barrel of a gun to the forehead of that man.

I hesitated asking him about Marika, or whoever she was. I was sure that he would answer, "Marika who? I knew of no Marika. Why do you ask?" I asked anyway. His answer was automatic, "Marika who? I knew of no Marika."

I angrily insisted, "It is impossible that you were not aware of an operation aimed at capturing a group of resistants at a supposed dropping site, in middle May, because she needed you and your men to carry it out."

The colonel took some time to answer, as if he was really digging deep into his memory. "I am sorry, sir," he finally said. "I have absolutely no memory of such an operation or of a woman named Marika."

Was it true? If it were, who was the so-called Marika? I looked one last time at a perfect gentleman soldier in a clean German uniform, a nice-looking man with white short hair and clean conscience, a man who did not seem too depressed by his actual situation. I felt tired and disgusted. I left.

For weeks, I refused to imagine what had been the fate of the six persons who had been "taken alive" by the "Gestapo."

It took time before "we," the underground army, were reintegrated into the French army. We kept on living in the woods, or at the edge of the woods, for a while. Some of our men evaporated, as if by enchantment. I suppose that they went back home without asking permission to do so. But so what? Eugene also went back home, promising that he would be back, and he came back. Marc and I remained in our little village.

Our first act of peace consisted of going to church the next Sunday. For the first time since D-Day, the bell rang. There were no longer several boys, more or less our age, attending mass, there was no longer a nice-looking girl with blond hair and green eyes leaning her bicycle against the right wall of the church, but Marc and I considered that it was the least we could do for Father Durand. Several couples of farmers attended, husbands and wives who previously came regularly, and also the two or three very young girls who disappeared as soon as they were out of church. My grandmother was there, wearing her beautiful "Italian straw hat" that two indefinite artificial flowers ornamented. After mass, contrary to her habit, she did not hurry home to prepare a Sunday lunch.

We were invited for that Sunday lunch by Marc's grandparents. A long table was set outside. We sat at the table in the company of Father Durand, Annette and P'tit Louis, farmer Georges, Bernadette, and their son, and Michelle's godfather and godmother. I had a few dramatic minutes with them. I told them that I loved Michelle and that she loved me. They said that they would always keep flowers, theirs and mine, on Michelle's tomb and that they would provide a stone after re-burying her. Then, we agreed that we should not spoil the pleasure of the others, and we joined them.

When night enveloped our clamorous assembly, we lighted oil lamps and the last candles of Father Durand's sacristy to end our evening with dignity. We parted after a last glass of wine, accepting the return invitations by Annette and P'tit Louis, farmer Georges, Bernadette, and their son, and Michelle's godfather and godmother in the coming days. My grandmother, Father Durand, and I would join forces to set our table in the courtyard of the school when it was our turn. I expected Father Durand to say something dramatic like, "And go to hell who breaks the promise!" but he did not. Promises are promises that must always be fulfilled. We did our part.

Furthermore, we fulfilled new promises, including many official banquets, until we were reintegrated into the army.

When we went back home, that night, my grandmother's hat was no longer on her head but in her hands. She repeated several times that this day happily erased in her mind some not-so-happy days of the recent past, and that she was ready to go for more any time.

My grandmother went back to Paris two weeks later. I missed her, her tranquil and loving presence, and her cool behavior. But life also had to go on. My parents, back in Paris, wanted her to join them. At the same time, Father Durand was given another parish, a larger one, far away from the village. By the time he left, nobody had opened "Marika's house."

When I left, Michelle's parents had not yet come back. I never went back myself to the "village."

Months later, still in the army with Marc, I received a message. A man named Daniel was arriving from a concentration camp. Could I pick him up at the railroad station? Marc and I went to the station. We knew of only one Daniel. I had never met him but Marc had on several occasions, and it was because of his arrest that we had decided to create a group of resistance to wage our own war against the Germans. When the train stopped, Marc only said, "That's him! The other car." Then he added, "Oh, God!"

Two nurses supported a man who had been young not so long ago, now an emaciated face and eyes surrounded by black shadows.

"Am I happy to see you!" he said with difficulty, articulating through toothless gums. We did not find the right words at the moment, and he saw our embarrassment. "Don't look at me like that," he said as if he wanted to excuse himself, "I'll be OK soon, and with new teeth. Yes, they tortured me to make me say what I knew about the resistance. I knew nothing, and I told them that I knew nothing. They tore my teeth one by one with a screwdriver to make me say what I knew about the resistance. I knew nothing, and nothing, and nothing. Even if I had been willing to talk, I had nothing to tell them. Which resistance? There was no resistance!"

When my brother Christian died in August 1983, his last words were, "Tell my brother Michel to bring me my red cap."

Made in the USA
Charleston, SC
26 February 2015